RELATION AMOUREUSE

AGAINST DOMESTIC VIOLENCE

A.J. Prince

authorHOUSE®

AuthorHouse™
1663 Liberty Drive
Bloomington, IN 47403
www.authorhouse.com
Phone: 1-800-839-8640

Published by AuthorHouse 11/16/12

ISBN: 978-1-4772-8984-6 (sc)
ISBN: 978-1-4772-8983-9 (e)

CONTENTS

V

VI

VII

VIII

IX

PART I

VERY TURBULENT RELATIONSHIPS

MISCONCEPTION ON THE DEFINITION OF LOVE *and* VIOLENCE IN RELATIONSHIPS

Reading a book may often be considered as a journey of change in the reader's life. It will be better be done by adopting the new concepts you will find in this book that are expressed by new.

Here they are:

Agaphobia = fear of love

Yeenaphobia = the fear of woman

DP = direct perception, dream

HBB = human being becoming

The Causality of Turbulent Relationships between Man and Woman

The two in relationships are young, unable to manage their feelings about the whole things called relationships between male and female.

They do not comprehend yet, the sexual apparatus, so they are sexually frustrated

One of the two does not expect to stay longer in the relationships, has hidden agenda

One of the two or the two are violent outside of the relationships.

One of the two or the two are neurotic or psychotic.

The woman is not sure of her "femininity" the man is not sure of his masculinity

Both have a big sense of inferiority

One of the two or the two have too much of a sense of worthlessness and incompleteness, that is to say they are asking too much out of love.

Mistreated at work or in life in general, the anger is directed toward the other partner. Or belittled at work they are on a revenge binge at home

One of the members of the relationships is in a stressful financial situation, has no money.

Love is not the real motivation of the relationships. It is money or social status.

One of the two is in a very high social status compared with the others.

Social violence, crime makes violence in love relationships an acceptable way to deal with issues

The man is a misogynist- women hater- ; the female is a man eater as would say Nelly Furtado

Absence of other kinds of love

We live in societies so disintegrated, meaning, in perpetual inner war, no wonder there are fights in men and women relationships.

The last possible cause of fight in men and women relationships, they so not love with each other.

The items in this part will appear in the rest of the book one way or another

The Idea that Being in Love is Detrimental to Success in Other Areas of Our lives

When I started to go out with women, the first issue I had to face was how to stay in love and be successful at the same time. I was young, thought it was because of lack of experience in the love department I was asking myself such questions. Then, later in life, the questions I thought that would disappear kept coming back. It's only now I realize that these sorts of questions need to be answered, for these solutions are part of what will create your success in relationships, what will make them lasting and fulfilling.

In the small village where I lived the first part of my life there was a girl who behaved like a HBB who had a crush on me. I was alone with her a couple times, but the relationships didn't last very long. For some reason I was not really interested in her romantically. Make sure he or she is really interested in you, otherwise you are pushing against a brick wall, could lead to fights or even murder.

When I moved to Port-au-Prince, the capital of Haiti, I met another girl Jeanine (was looking a little bit like Whitney Houston and like Paris), the same first name than the previous one, in whom I was not really interested. So with her everything should have gone well. However it was not the case. After a few months in the relationships, I was quarrelling with her often enough. One day I hit her, she fell unconscious for a few seconds. For sometimes I thought that lack of confidence, jealousy in myself were the only two causes of my behaviour. True, I spent a lot of time with her and neglected the work I was doing. The fact that her aunt was living close to the school where I was teaching didn't help the matter, for she spent most of my times there, neglecting school work

I hit her because I was raised in a violent society, where violence is perceived as having a great value. I hit her, because I thought she would love me more. It was a childish conception of love, but that was the way I was brought up, the way it is still for millions of other HBBs in the world nowadays.

One of my nephews said to me once that he doesn't play around in his office and he doesn't try to get closer to any woman in the office. His desk is clean; there is absolutely nothing on top of it. All in all he was trying to tell me that it is the way to keep working when we have a job. I didn't have time to analyze what he said, didn't have time to tell him that it is the way he is going to fail if not at his work, but surely as a person. For the fundamentals are not there, liking and loving other HBBs no matter what, no matter where is more likely to get us succeed.

He lost one job immediately after 9/11 (I had to shake him up mentally to make him find another one), I thought he would make a tight link between the two, 9/11 and the lost job. He didn't make the link after all, was rather thinking that the lost of the job was related to something in him, love and liking like as I thought, for his work ethics are too tight.

Lack of Formal Education and the Tanks of Love

Sometimes, I have the impression that some of my own brothers can't differentiate between familial love and sexual love- idea which still floating in Freudian psychology. I had a tendency to attribute the deficiency to lack of schooling. It is the only feature that is obvious in them as it is related to the sexual discrimination absence of it. But after hearing the song on Lucas, an adolescent living in an upper floor of a building complaining of sexual assault on the part of her parent in North America, I am no longer so sure that I was dealing only with lack of education. Apparently at the beginning marriage was done in the family , that psychic awakening brings with it erotic awakening. What can cause mental disorder which in its turn can create fight in relation between man and woman?

I do not want to bring incest on the table. It becomes a taboo and it can be very controversial. But it, too, does reflect an incapacity to differentiate many kinds of love (fraternal love, the Creator's love), despite what Freud had said on it.

Human species would not survive for long if sexual love between members of same family became a common practice over a long period of time. We would all be killed by diseases, because the pull of genes would be too homogeneous to be able to fight all the possible diseases.

It might be Doctor Phil who wrote it, it was presented on Oprah once. It is on the tanks of love. The book describes at least 10 kinds of love such as sexual love, parental love, sibling love, friendly love, the Creator's love, etc. There is a simple prescription in the book. One tank of love is full, you have to leave it aside for a while, and pass to another tank of love which by that time became empty (another activity related to love). I think that it can help anyone to find himself in the ethereal field that we call love, at the same time it helps dissipate the thinking that there is one kind of love. We will fight if we think like that because it is not true.

The Macho Syndrome

Passionate love was a way of life for me. I didn't go out with many women, but I went out with only one at a time, then, it was an intensive love. At the same time the macho kind of love was always in the air- still now what is present paradigm in Hollywood. When friends and I gathered together, something I did quite often adolescent and young adult, we talked regularly about men who have made many feminine conquests. We admire those men. We thought they were inculcated with some kind magic sense to sweep the feet of any beautiful woman, to change them into love slave. In other words I thought these men were very successful in love.

Then, when I started reading psychology books, I started to see "l'envers du décors" (the other side of the decorum), I started to realize that instead of being successful, these men were miserable, and where failing in love, the reason why they went from one woman to the other, that if they were

7

succeeding in love they would stay put with one of them. At least they would not go from one to the other like a grasshopper, like a butterfly, from one flower to the other.

I thought that character, as Don Juan was the value in regard to love at a certain time in human history. How many of you are still thinking the same way? Now I am not going out with a woman for reasons pertinent only to me. When I was active in the domain, I met women very often. I was almost certain that many men and women are doing the same experience, that is to say, when they are already going out with a woman or a man, they meet potential partner almost every day, but when they are not in love it becomes difficult for them to meet a single probable partner.

There is an explanation to the phenomenon. It is because Don Juan type of a person is a value in love for most of us, men and women, although deep down of things he is a bore, the biggest failure in love as they say. Not knowing that is bound to get us in trouble in 'relation amoureuse"

A Little Bit on the Definition of Love

It is not clear to me why it is not easy for every HBB to have at least this conception about the definition of love. *It is in general a bundle of positive emotions.* We all know when we are in love, but most of us wouldn't be able to put it in terms so simple. We probably are too emotional about it in the first place (like in music, we remember the song; we like the son but rarely remember all the words. We are too much in love to understand love. Understanding requires reflection, a return into one's psyche, one self. In love we are rather most of the time thinking about the beloved, very little about ourselves, even less about thing, even love itself.

If you didn't make that conclusion after reading the paragraph above, it is referring to romantic love, which is a little bit like love in general, but in a more intensive fashion. Lovers in romantic love are rapped around each other, forgetting almost everybody, everything else. Swan a character of Marcel Proulst said something like love is the only one thing that makes his life meaningful.

The concept of love hasn't been easy to master, is not a simple matter (Can we touch a feeling, our love?) in the intellectual world either and it has been this way from the beginning of man and woman kind history to now. In psychological literature, there are many approaches, and theories on love. In his book Motivation Theories and Principles Fourth Edition, Robert C. Beck mentioned some of them. According to him and Freud love is a modified version of sexuality. Love occurs because sex is repressed. Maslow distinguishes D love or deficiency love from lack of feeling of security, belonging; love or being loved from the desire for self-actualization. For Robin love and liking are overlapping, liking based on affection and respect, love based on attachment caring and intimacy. Davis starts from liking (friendships), enjoyment, mutual assistance, spontaneity, acceptance, trust, understanding and confidence; finishes with loving: all the elements of liking plus passion, sexual desire, exclusiveness, and caring (surrendering).

In that context romantic lovers are monogamous, not so much for ideological reason, but simply because lovers in romantic love have very little time left for themselves in separate activities, to take care of themselves, for example. So, they don't have time to include other lovers in the equation.

Everyone goes about living his life not questioning the misconceptions about love, however these misconceptions do have negative consequence on relationships, on love, on couple in love, do play a role in violence in couples in relationships.

Other Definitions of Love

In his book *Love and the World,* Robert Sadello wrote note necessarily in the same format:

We have exploited love as:

    -an image

    -a force in the world

    -an emotion

    -a knowledge of oneself

-an action in the heart

-a world phenomena

-a form in the world

-a mysterious force among HBBs

-the essence

-the essence of the world itself, it substance being an activity and destiny

Elsewhere he wrote again............ that "loving is the same as being ever more aware of the world as an activity in which the I is engaged".

Again:............. "For love means establish intimate relationship with the not known"............

A Bit on the Cause of Love-We love the person who we think loves us or we love her because we think she has something we value. There might be lots more other ways why we love the other person; those two are the most common.

II

THE FUNCTIONS OF SEXUAL FRUSTRATION
and
BRUTALITY IN COUPLES
IN RELATIONSHIPS

Before the functions of sexual frustrations itself, it would be better may be to say a few words about the functions of fights on relationships themselves, for most of them are to and will destroy relationships. They first destroys **contact** (exchange of thoughts and feelings via communication) between the two members of the couple in liaison, or at the beginning it was the fights, later the two members of the couple in love but at war with each other become "uncommunicado" At this moment, then, starts the undoing of the relationships. All in all "Relation Amoureuse" is to promote the evolvement of love and relationships in couples (not much to say on that, it destroys it). That is why we would not be able to develop the function of fights on relationships.

Lack of Knowledge on Woman Anatomy and on Sexual Mechanism

Jeanine and I had a lot of good times together. As said above, I spent a lot of lunch times with her at her aunt's, times I should use preparing afternoon classes. Nonetheless, what I adored doing with her was to go to a beach where I rented a small cabin (a little shed), and spent time with her. It was very hot. We spent part of time in the shed, the other part in the sea swimming.

The thing is we had many intimate moments, but it was always without going all the way, She didn't want to get pregnant at the wrong time, so she was a bit uptight. However, the main reason why it was like that I think, was because I was very much so inexperienced in the sexual relation domain. I didn't have a firm idea on thing such as pubic bone, the rest of the feminine sexual apparel. It is why we didn't go all the way, for I wanted it so much, and I had the impression that she wanted it as well at the bottom of things.

It was not the first time I faced the same problem (not knowing how to go all the way), and it is clear to me that other young men had to do the same negative experience. How would I be so sure of knowing such a thing? Here it is, I was going out with Mireille off and on in Montreal. She said to me that once she met an Italian guy, they were or wanted to be intimate, but he didn't succeed in going all the way. She argued that the sexual apparel of the Italian guy was too big, but I concluded that he did know how to go all the way, as it happened to me in the first of my experiences in the matter.

So, it is not astonishing to say that the quarrels I was having with Jeanine were strongly motivated by sexual frustration. Not really because we didn't have sex all the way, but because we went so close and didn't finish it.

Boredom

Boredom in couple in relationships is what triggered the idea "Relations Amoureuses" for it is what I come to conclude after observing Arnold and Anne Marie's relationships. Arnold is one of my brothers. He married

Anne Marie's quite a long time ago. They have many children: Marie Sony, Cathia, Ingreed, Nick and Jeffrey. For them to be married for so long and to have so many children together would mean that their marriage is a success. But it is not, there were many fights and quarrels in it all along the years they were living together. I am not quite sure if they are faithful to each other in their relationships. Presently Arnold is living in Florida, Anne Marie is in New York.

Obviously there was something that kept them together for so long. He was always talking to me about it when their kids were very young, I always told him that he had to keep it together with his wife for the sake of the kids. But I definitely don't think that that what kept them together. Love should have been the reason they staid together.

If they have been in love with each other, why the quarrels and the fights? Why did they choose to use the negative, violent and destructive way of communicating their love for each other?

They were bored with themselves each separately and with each other. They didn't go to movies, to theatre, to concert together. They didn't read books, didn't receive friends, so no social life. Very early in the relationships, each Sunday afternoon Arnold used to open a small radio that plaid music that his wife, his kids and him self listened to. That was the only entertainment they had together.

They were bored and were desperately trying to find a way to communicate with each other to alleviate their boredom

First of all he should have loved more (a hobby) than his wife and his kid. Second of all, he should have entertained himself and his family a lot more. This way, he would keep filling up many tanks of love when they are empty, as suggested in the first chapter. This way, he would find a better canal of communication with his wife than the one they used to use together, that is to say quarrels and fights, the dangerous zone

They both didn't go to school much. The lack of education may have contributed to the restriction in entertainment field and the canals of communication.

The negative communication itself was fuelling their boredom and the boredom was fuelling the negative communication. We don't come out of the wood yet.

"Ritualization" of Ambivalence: An inadequate Mode of Communication

Ritualization of ambivalence is when two HBBs are in a durable "relation amoureuse" and that they quarrel and fight most of the time. It is to understand that after a while in relationships, love, as exciting it was at the beginning, might take a retreat. Lovers are not so much into each other anymore. The aspect of newness is no longer there after time together the taste and the colour of the relationships become dull and "blasés". We understand that to avoid these moments, and/or to cross them without any damage to the "relationships, negative expression is installed. The negative expression becomes one side of the ambivalence (are we in love or are we not); in other words, the negative expression is staged.

Sometimes, those kinds of love last very long. Those kinds of lovers may even have grand children. As a way to communicate love, "ritualisation of ambivalence" however, doesn't seem to be a sure technique for a fulfilling life for lovers themselves, their children and their friends? Young children may be very disturbed by surprising their parents "in bed" let alone seeing them unhappily arguing or fighting. Even adults, other members of family and friends are not pleased by witnessing constant arguments between couples. Even myself personally I felt very bad when I noticed Arnold and Anne Marie arguing one more time. I thought that they might have felt very bad inside, that it was not going to end and that it was a drain on the creative potential of all the members of that family.

Furthermore, there is this little knowledge in psychology according to which underneath of any feeling lies its opposite, under love lies hate. In this context, "ritualisation" of ambivalence is playing with fire because it may reach the hatefulness underneath the love relationship. Then, there can be some skidding which brings the lovers to violence, and even to lives destruction.

It is not because of any doctrine that I am trying to understand violence in couples in relationships, nor a hidden agenda. You are doing it purely because of the possibility of skidding. If each time couples argue, after that it stops there, then there would be no reason to be so interested in the subject. Even in the hand of experts in emotional control setting, "ritualization" of ambivalence may skid directly toward death. In that sense it's not necessarily promoting life, but it may destroy it.

All in all installing negative expression for "ritualisation" of ambivalence creates the risk of the lost control and degeneration into negative action. Lovers kill themselves many times.

Drug

It's as if one woman I was going out with could detect when I have been drinking at hundred miles from her. She was so accurate in her detection of alcohol in my breath that I didn't drink at all when I was about to meet her, to go to her place. It was like that, but I didn't know what the fuss about drinking alcohol was about. For at that time, I was only an occasional drinker, at that period of my life I drank rather at parties, I was a social drinker. It was only after the failure of the relationships, I discovered that there was a link between consumption of alcohol and decrease of sexual appetite.

She was wearing a black dress; she was sitting at a table with some friends at the Shark Club. She looked nice and attractive. My heart was pumping under the resonance of the sounds of the loud music and at the view of a woman I liked and who smiled at me. That had encouraged me to talk her a bit. However, during that time I was not going out with anyone, and used to drink quite a bit. Before I went to the shark club I was at hotel Georgia for the afternoon drinking on a Friday night. I didn't really know what I was saying to her. After a few minutes, the "love affair" with her ended. She had probably noticed that I was pissed drunk.

The hotel in which the club was located on Sherbrook Street in Montreal. We met right after I arrived at the place, as if I had a date with her. Linda was from Toronto and she was visiting Montreal for the night. It is not clear if it was because I was so pleased with her, but in the space of an hour I had already gulped many bottles of wine. I was very drunk. I was not even driving, but that night I had to drive her to my place, for she was too drunk to do it herself. "Comme-ci, comme-ca" I drove home with her. I went to bed right away, after finding her a pyjamas. I felt asleep immediately afterward. She woke early the day after, dressed went outside and left to go back to Toronto. I failed to interest her in sexuality and love, because of alcohol.

It would be possible to bring up front many similar cases where alcohol has prevented me from being intimate with a woman, then in relationships with women. In itself, it could be seen as a banality. In couple in relationships, if the two members are like that, it bounds to create sexual frustration, if one member is like that, it, again, will create sexual frustration. It has been seen above that sexual frustration can cause violence in couple.

Most of other types of drug have the same negative effect in relationships than alcohol if not worse.

Phobia

It was a surprise for me when I learn that phobia can be inherited. It has been discovered that children born in cities are not afraid of snakes, becoming adults, all of a sudden they have the phobia of snake. No wonder that fear plays such an important part in HBBs misery. Fear plays a part in the causality of almost all our "failures" in life. When we have a goal, encounter some difficulty in the process of creating it, phobia certainly lie underneath crippling our creative skills, when our desires are not fulfilled, we are victim of the same unconscious disabling process.

So here are 2 techniques currently used to get off phobia in general:

The psychoanalytic tried treatment would focus on finding the underlying conflict or source to anxiety leading the phobia and on reducing that anxiety.

Modifying Fear

One treatment called systematic desensitization is to present a phobic stimulus (a snake in rubber) repeatedly to a patient, showing that it has no ill effect and hopefully producing its extinction. This treatment is usually done in conjunction with fear hierarchy, gradually presenting a client with stimuli that are progressively more similar to the phobic stimulus.

New Phobia

I spent 10 years without love, without even touching a woman (I am hetero) involuntarily. The following are new kind of phobia discovered by me governing the compulsive behavior:

1. "Aga-phobia" — Phobia or the Fear of Love

Why a relatively mentally and physically healthy HBB has such a phobia? A psychoanalyst would ask to go in the person infancy life to find out the source of "Aga" phobia However to explain any phobia; we can always start by the person lack of history related to the phobia in question. "Agaphobia" is then caused by lack of history in the field of love. In plain language, it means our friend has never been loved (sexually and otherwise) and has never loved someone else before.

It does happen to adolescents and young adults who have the age when most of very important experiences of live begin. I have been the beloved in this bizarre experience many times. In other words, they love me, they come at the place where I am, but never say a word. A girl I called Cinthia did it at least a dozen at the branch Dunbar of the Vancouver Public Library during at least four or five years. In French, we would say "le chat a mordu sa langue", the cat has bitten her tongue. Apparently it's common phenomenon in adolescent and young adult life. Phenomenon, because we all know very well that at this age, we are very talkative. When, I was teaching classes from elementary to high School, sometimes I say Blah! Blah! Blah! Very loudly the students quit talking and get them ready for the class.

Aga-phobia does exist.

Nonetheless in certain cases adult and less young HBBs do the same experience. In other words, they may have or have been never loved sexually before. There are priests, sisters, sick HBBs, HBBs born with part of their body not functioning or even absent. Those HBBs may experience agaphobia also.

2. "Atoma" — Phobia or the Fear of Men from Women

If there is yeenaphobia (fear of women from men, see below), there is no reason for not having equally atomaphobia, but it may be experienced differently:

There is the fact that men are physically stronger than women are in most cases. It is a cause for men phobia.

There are misogynous men such as Lepine who crime on a number of women in Montreal and the one who kill a Woman at Dawson College in the same city recently. They are cause for "atomaphobia" in women.

There are polygamous men.

There is what is wrongly called bigamy when one man marries twice. Wrongly named, because these men marry not just two women at a time, but many. In court the third marriage is legal for not being a bigamy, another reason for "atomaphobia" in women. They have many women so they are not committing a bigamy and cannot be bugged by the law. What about the cause for a laugh.

There are men who are in a period of violence in their lives. There are serial killers like Picton, Olson.

So, although I am not a woman, it's not totally obscure to my being how women experience the fear of men.

Nowadays, there are the rape pills, one more reason for "atoma-phobia

All those phobia are bound to cause frustration and violence in couples in relationships.

3. "Egkumosunè" — Phobia or Pregnancy Fear

In one advertisement on TV the women explain a little bit why they are afraid of getting pregnant. One woman says that her boyfriend said he would leave her if she gets pregnant. Another adds that her boss would fire her. Those reasons may be related to modern time, a bad sign for the well being of the relationships.

However, this fear is of an all time phobia.

In the past they used to find new babies in front of a church, or somewhere where the baby could be found. I think I've seen in film in which the baby was wrapped in waterproof piece of linen and thrown to the river. The baby was found by someone else far away down the river. Recently a baby was left somewhere in Toronto. After one or two days of noise about it in the media the mother identified herself. Actually it iis an event that occur quite regularly.

Why?

Poverty would not be at the source of the fear, for the poor countries in the world make more children.

Among the reasons at the bottom of fear of getting pregnant, social stigma is the biggest or the most obvious. In some places in the world it is a capital sin to have a baby before marriage in the time past and now too. Even myself young adult I was among those who thought it is no good to get pregnant before marriage. When I saw one of my sisters being pregnant without being married, I was not very happy at all..

4. "Eomeuoe" — Phobia or Fear of Commitment

In psychology there is what is called the cost of value, and one of the parameters of the topic is when we choose one course of action instead other courses of action. In other words when we choose one course of action, we eliminate many other courses of action. Is it one reason behind the fear of commitment, that we don't want to eliminate many eliminate too many courses of actions, that we would like to keep all the courses action, That we would like to keep the cake and eat it too? It can make things a bit unsound.

There is the question, also, as to "have we made the good choice for us or not? One of the reasons why I am not in relationships nowadays is the fear of commitment. I do not want to enter into relationships with women who are not among the ones I would like to have children with, for in those relationships I would have to commit sometimes. I do not want to commit with the wrong woman for me.

I went out with Debbie for 6 years. I did not commit in this relationships, because, first of all she was separate but not divorced. If I was about to marry her, she would have to get a divorce from the previous husband. Here comes the second point: I did not propose to her for feeling that the teacher on call work I was doing at that time were not stable enough to get married on it. Another reason I did not ask to marry her was because I did not think she was interested in getting married a second time. When I found out she was interested and was going to ask her to marry me, then she started to behave strangely. Finally, I broke up with her, after I found another man in her apartment.

She was not really the woman I wanted to get children with, but after going out with her for so many years, I said to myself that she became the one, that there was not really good reason not to confirm the relationships with her socially.

So a lot of feelings may come into play in regard to fear of commitment in couple relationships, but the most common one seems to be related to the matcho syndrome which was the object of our discourse previously. Most HBBs, it seems, have the fear of commitment for thinking consciously or not that it is better to be in relationships with many opposite partners at a time. The thought may be unconscious, but sure to be there, for it is a value in many societies, from the night of time to now. The matcho type personality is wrongly valued, it disguises failure, or in it failure is taken for success. Nonetheless the matcho type personality is sure to fuel the fear of commitment from men. We could even say that it is the fear of commitment itself.

Some psychologists would explain it by sexual trauma at one point in the person life, as tape, forceful consignment for sexual activities and so on.

5. "Oikelotèta" — Phobia or the Fear of Intimacy

Itself can be caused by the fear of pregnancy. This fear is in the heart of violence in couple, for impairing sexual activity in the couple if not preventing it from happening totally. Obviously young couples are the ones who can be the victim of this kind of fear, assuming that less younger couples have the time to master the art of birth control (For one reason or another, another women I was going out with made me used a couple of times the withdrawal technique. (Oh boy! Sexual activity has never been so exciting).

As said at the beginning of the chapter, Jeanine was very concerned of getting pregnant at the wrong time, for she was not using any birth control device.

And most of the fears have under them a lack of history in the matter plus other causes. It is the same for the fear of intimacy. Of course, adolescents and young adults have this fear. In the case of adolescent it is a good things, they are not in our topic anyway for they are not suppose to be among couples in sexual relationships. However, the fear of intimacy disturbs couples of all ages from young adults to less younger ones. It happens for many reasons.

Amanda was roommate, a beautiful woman. She initiates sexual relationships with me a couple of times. I didn't have sexual relation with her. Sometimes I was taken by surprise. At that time I was living on amount of money too little to feed myself. Most of the time I was hungry and preoccupied by my feedings.

When Amanda was about to move out, I had a date with her hoping we would make up for the time lost in intimacy. That night the water heater was broken all of a sudden. Before that she took a bath everyday.

Heather was a previous roommate; I could have made love with her, also. I did not.

What was at work in all the missed opportunities to make love in the above paragraphs is the fear of intimacy. I think that the fear of intimacy for me is itself caused by the fact that I haven't made love for a while (a few years). In other cases fear of intimacy can be the result of personal belief, a wrong assumption on sexuality. If I think that it's not a good idea to make love before marriage, then, I will develop the "oikelotèta" phobia, which would prevent me from keeping my partners.

They were also wreckful sexual opportunities

6. "Sexonalikez Astheueiez" — Phobia the Fear of Sexual Diseases

May also appear in couples where one or both partners have the fear of sexual diseases. Especially after the arrival of AIDS in the field of sexual diseases dictionaary. This fear is a very potent one. It can not only prevent intimacy in couples in relationships, but also prevent the formation of the couple in the first place. That's why it is to be mentioned under the topic of phobia in couples. In other words, when fear of sexual disease is not an impediment to the formation of couple it is a cause for sexual frustration, then, violence in couple's relationships, the title of this chapter.

7. "Uamoz" — Phobia or the Fear of Marriage

This fear is very similar to the fear of commitment, but not necessarily the same, for some HBBs (As Jean Paul Sartre was) don't agree with marriage as a social concept, but do commit in relationships that last a long time.

The fear of marriage reminds me of Paul. There was a deformity in one of his legs. So he did not walk as everyone else. The day he was about to get married, all the guests and his future wife to be were waiting, But Paul was no where to be found. After looking for him a while, Paul was seen on top of a coconut tree near by. I used to laugh to the point of loosing consciousness when I remember what Paul did, hidden on top of a coconut tree in order not to get married. It is so, so funny but illustrates well Uamoz"-phobia or the fear of marriage.

In life in general HBBs will come up with all sorts of excuses in order not to get married, but the reality is that the fear of marriage is quite common in human life. Many times a marriage is about to happen, all of a sudden, one member of the couple is no where to be found, strange but real, and is also a major cause of violence in couples in relationships. The subject is well known in Hollywood.

8. "Yeena" — Phobia

Is the fear of women, not to confuse with misogyny: the hate of women.

Rhona, the psychotherapist who had a show in the radio of the same name used to ask first if they have sisters to the callers who questioned her on how to meet women. That was a common question on her shows, meaning that yeenaphobia also is more common than we could imagine. Before living in Vancouver, and even at the beginning of my life in Vancouver I used to go out with a woman very often. Not being in this kind of relationships since 1998 (now we are in 2005), I become very uncomfortable with women in general, especially with women I find attractive. I have, "yeena"-phobia, for being heterosexual and being not physically sick, or psychotic, sexual relation with women is in my mind all the time. "Yeena"-phobia becomes part of the explanation as to why I do not have one yet.

The bus let me down, a woman and I were in the dark at a bus stop near a little forest. The bus was going to garage; we had to wait for another UBC bus. Although I was tempted to talk to her, instead, I staid 10 feet away from her in order not to create fear in her in this special circumstance, but at the bottom of things I was suffering of yeenaphobia, I was acting under the push of yeenaphobia, for it was an opportunity to strike a conversation with her and find out if she is available for relationship or not.

Manipulation of Love for Economic Purposes

Last Monday was Valentine day, the day of love, the way you say it. On TV they show a Student saying that that day is Hallmark Day. In other words Valentine day was created for economic purposes, to sell Hallmark Cards. Right afterward, it was showed also a professor who said that student are always protesting, that Valentine defied a roman law which interdicted marriage of Young men who were needed for war. Valentine was in jail; February 14 was when he sent a card to his wife from the jail cell. The professor was demonstrating that February 14 is a good day to celebrate love. He did well, don't you think?

But the manipulation of love (and sexuality) for economic purposes, the point brought by the student may not apply in the case of Valentine day, but do apply in other cases. In market economy lesser is better most of the time. Society may make of love a rare object by placing a lot of does and don'ts on it in order to make it difficult to obtain for the sake of value (scarcity for value). Imagine everyone is in love, no one goes in clubs at night looking for an especial soul sister, looking for love. Nightclub owners would be ruined.

The capitalist economic system in general made its mark as being the better than the communist economic system. One idea in the communist philosophy is the dictatorship by the people. Some governments in some countries use the idea even if they do not officially declare themselves as being communist. They become dictators in those countries and used violence to keep the dictatorship alive), but both communism and capitalism have valuable and invaluable elements, and in the market economy, too, there is potential for violence, a source of violence in couple relationships.

I found out lately that the communist thinkers, although the bigger parts of their economic theories are wrong, In the deep down they also have big humanist feelings. They would like to see a most of us if not all of us, have descent, more authentic life .

The same goes for the business HBBs (employers) also. At first we think they are in it for the money. Worst they themselves are thinking like that too. But deep down they have passion for humanity, for human being well being.

Let us come back to our lambs. Poverty is the first to come to mind. Some how there is a place for it in this kind of economy, and it's sure is a potential for violence. It is one of the reasons why welfare have been created, to keep the poor HBBs away from becoming violent against the rich HBBs who are living in the same cities, same areas than poor HBBs sometimes.

Then there is the syndicate to counter balance the power of corporations. They stop working in order to protest against a decision of a corporation, or to claim what they think is theirs but not given to them by the corporation. Protestation is more or less a violent action. Sometimes HBBs get kill during protesting action.

The point is that at work there is stress that creates the conditions for violence in couples in relationships. The point is that when HBBs don't have paying jobs, that creates potential for violence in couples in relationships. The point is that even at work there is violence that one or both partners drag at home with themselves and which permeates their relationships.

The Absence of Inner Relationships

"I never dreamt at night" was what the editor said to me after reading the step on that HBBs might use their dreams at night to tell them how best to quit smoking in a book I call Kickwell Or Else and that I want to publish. I was so surprised, for I thought before meeting him that all HBBs; especially intellectual HBBs have dreams. Then, if he thinks that he doesn't dream, relationships with the unconscious part of him, with his unconscious self is at point 0, serious handicap to his relationships to his partner, cause for violence in his relationships with his partner

Of course we all dream at night, but after a day full of activities, announcing a tomorrow equally full of activities, we may not notice our dreams at night, if we believe dreams have no value whatsoever, we may not notice our dream. I we believe dream does not exist, we are going to miss them in our psyche. There is a link between psychic revelation and sexual revelation. Someome who is not in contact with his psyche has erotic problem, does not have intimacy as such, not a high point for relationships.

Dreams are not the only way we relate to our selves. There is meditation, self talk.

Inner relationships is the most important activities of HBBs, but not the easiest one. The way we are born physically facing the world is not really encouraging us to look back at ourselves. It easier to look at someone else whom we can see without the help of any instrument. To look at ourselves we need the help of a mirror. Fortunately, wanting it or not, we relate to ourselves unconsciously, although it's at this stage it's a natural, underdeveloped, bare bone kind of self-relationships.

So, it is more likely we will spend our lives with one part of ourselves fighting against the other, and the inner struggle is bound to be reflected in other areas of our lives, in our relationships with others, if we are able to have some of it in the first place, in couples in relationships.

Abstraction on "Feminity" and Masculinity

1. Men Have to Be Strong

"Men have to be strong" is what is believed in most societies on this planet nowadays and may be from the night of time. Why do we think it has to be so? I am seriously curious about the origin of the idea, although you bet that it is one of the "children" of the naturalist school from the time of Darwin. For it is known that where comes from another bizarre idea "survival of the fittest". Anyway, "Men have to be strong" implies that women have to be weak. This thought must have been evolved from the observation that men are physically of more voluminous than women are in general. From there it is concluded that they have to be stronger than women are mentally and physically. Actually, it means only that men have to be strong mentally, for no one would say men are stronger than women are physically. It would be a pleonasm.

For example, when I was going to college in Montreal, I've met Georgette, one the most beautiful women in the world. She was already a nurse, working in a hospital. I loved her very much, but made so many mistakes in the relationships with her that after about a year with her, one day she packed her bags and moved out to a building for woman in the city, until she founds a permanent place to stay, I guess. I went to her new accommodation only once immediately after she left me in an apartment on Villeray Street in Montreal where I was living with her.

It's not necessary to go in all the details of the relationships, but I think the main reason why the relationships failed was the belief that men have to be stronger than women are. First of all, I didn't have a car; she had an old one. At that time, I used to go to New York very often. One-day time was up to go there again. She said she would go with me in her car. So, we did go to that city, spent a few days there, visiting my brothers and their families. Then, we went back to Montreal.

The mistake was that I was very mad at her, because we were lost a little bit before reaching Brooklyn where one of my brothers were living at that time. She did drive all the way down there with me. Instead of thanking her many times for being so gracious, I was mad at her. No, I was not really mad at her, I was mad at myself for feeling so weak, for not having even a driver's license to help her to drive to go to New York. I felt really so weak, because of the idea that I am a man, I have to be stronger than her, and do the harder task that was driving t to New York, although I didn't have a driver's license. That's really why I was mad at her.

Second, I had a friend named Jean Claude who was married and who told me to keep a relationships, man has to be strong and show it to the woman by forcing her to do things for him when he want it to be done. Boy! I was so stupid then. One day she just arrived from work, I forced her to have sexual relation with me. It was almost like raping her. Imagine raping a woman who is already living with me. Can there be something more stupid than that? I had to show to her that I was the man in the relationships, she left, I lost. I was young.

Now, we have a problem, because there is nothing to justify the requirement that men have to be stronger then women mentally, and nothing to make us believe that men are able to be stronger then women mentally speaking. Another overgeneralization from misreading life(because we turn our face away from the Creator), that enters into the equation of violence in couples in relationships.

All that would mean men cannot really love women, for the stronger man image would prevent them from surrendering essential ingredient of love, especially of romantic love.

2. Men without a Self/Women Oppression

In psychological literature, statistics show that the great majority of psychics are women. It is like dealing with the psyche, making the use of the psyche to give others insights on themselves, guiding them to do the right thing at the right time should be the work of a woman. A man psychic doesn't sound good, doesn't sound masculine enough.

Who knows, the fact that I had a great deal of difficulty in having a friend who is a man nowadays, for all the men I met took me for an homosexual or they were just looking for an homosexual, or they want to apply dictatorships in relationships. The reason why I had to eliminate their access to me. The situation itself may be related to the research I am doing on the psyche. The thing that the men find strange in me, that make me look not like a heterosexual for them may be my constant dealing with the psyche. They're may be transference love also.

A man is not supposed to have an intuition. We say of a woman that she is intuitive, but saying of a man that he is intuitive will not be well taken, makes the man looks like a homosexual. Intuition is the domain of women.

All these abstractions on the masculinity of men are bound to have a negative impact on the young men and prevent them from developing their inner world, prevent them from having a self. The self we are born with is like in a cocoon. For it to develop, we have to make an effort in understanding the psyche, our inner world. If there is stigma attached to men as related to the psyche, it would make it so that men do not develop in this particular domain. In these circumstances men will relate to themselves and others with great difficulty. This state of affairs may be responsible for violence in couples in relationships and wars. In other words, inner relationships is absent (Men are directed toward power and dominance or the fear of helplessness grows into the search for power and dominance of men. It becomes a social value that even women accepts, although, to all practical ends it means the oppression of women). The absence is against nature, creates predisposition for violence, which is only waiting for the right circumstances to develop in full motivation for violence in couples in relationships.

3. Alienation

As for all the other difficulties in life, they have many apparent sources. But anyone, who scratches a little bit deeper, will find alienation at the bottom. By alienation we mean when one part of the self is completely negating the other part (the ego negating the I, body, soul, spirit are not in tandem). HBBs affected by alienation do not say they are like that, sometimes may be not even conscious on that they are like that, but their behaviour left no doubt on their inner negation and deprivation. For them only the material world exists. For these HBBs what you see is what you get, nothing else in between, nothing else exists. A little bit like extremism in religion (and all kind of extremist HBBs as a matter of fact), but at the other side of the spectrum. For them, only the spiritual world exists, nothing else. In complete life, (in comparison to the incomplete life) translated by negation of life, by suicide, by war, by negating friendship, love. It is translated by violence in couple in relationships.

The Internet and the Chat Rooms

In itself the computer is one of the nicest piece of equipment HBBs have created for themselves. It allows us to be able to do numerous calculations, have bigger and more efficient companies. It spares us of tedious daily labor as it used to be before the creation of the machine. However, the nice toy brings with it also all sorts problems. If left alone, they will develop and cancel the benefits that the machine brings in our lives. On TV it was saying how many pornographic sites there are in the Internet in the last week of February 2005. I wanted to pay attention to be able to keep the exact number; there was a force in life greater than what was wanted and which was competing for my attention also. I fell asleep and didn't see the show after all.

Any way, it is clear for all of us that contact between HBBs via internet has an effect on relationships between men and women that cannot be measured to its full extent yet, but is sure to modify the interaction between them. It is clear for all of us that nowadays more children have been disappearing after having been chatting in the internet rooms with adult stranger who met them somewhere afterward, kidnapped them and did with them whatever purpose they had in mind before the kidnapping. In a couple therapy session John expressed the anger he felt watching his wife busy communicating with barely known individuals to her while he himself is left alone without some one to talk to. He said that in the house he spent most of his time with cans of beer. At the end of the session John promised to seek anger management help.

I thought that his marriage was about to be broken and wished that it didn't happen to them, for I didn't know if his wife will be able to stop chatting in the Internet, consequently if John will be able to control his anger. I hope that his anger doesn't change into violence against his wife.

Importance of Sexuality

How important is sexuality in life? Some psychologists would say that life is sexuality itself (How about Freud?). They say that men think of women each few minutes during a day, that "sex sells". Some HBBs spend most of their time thinking of sexuality, other HBBs spend most of their time doing it. Young men lust on sexual pictures making sexual material a big industry in North America if not in the whole world. Life continues on earth sexually.

So, sexuality is very important in life in general, and in most HBBs life, despite of what some religious groups would like you to believe.

Devastating Consequences of Sexual Frustration

It seems that violence especially in young couples is rather the consequences of sexual frustration. In many cases in life, when we are frustrated, we keep going at it until we succeed, or we withdraw from the task that we can't achieve and that frustrates us, with no major consequences in the short and long term basis. But with sexual frustration, it seems things do not just stop right there. There are ramifications in the short and in the long-term basis, and there is amplification as well.

I find out that sexual frustration of the men who used to live in the same house than me may have plaid a role in the death of two nephews, Eddy and Allan, that I had, and in the shooting of another one, Genio. He was shot on the back by a criminal who was wearing a balaclava, was brought to hospital where the extracted the bullet that was lodged in his back.

The reason I make the connection between the homosexual frustration and the death of Eddy and the shooting on Genio is that they are both nephews that I named at birth and because I was and am doing experiment in telepathy. Oh! Oh! Something went wrong and it is deadly. They are living 1000 miles away from me. The homosexuals who lived in the same house than me did not even know that I have nephews living thousand miles away from me let alone knowing them personally, so telepathy, the long distance experimentation must have plaid a role.

I did not name Allan, I did not make a connection between his death and the sexual frustration of the homosexual men who lived in the same house than me, but I link his death to another kind of sexual frustration. Again linked to the experimentation in telepathy. It is still an on going experimentation. The results are not all collected yet.

Not only it's a step made in the unknown, so mistakes may be made easily, but also the dead nephews had a weak personality, or had something wrong in their personality which made them do things that they should not have done and that caused their death plusn that political turnmoil was at its paroxysm, in the final analysis. The sexual frustration of HBBs around me would have plaid only a part in their death. I have other nephews, nothing happened to them. They have a stronger personality.

III

SOCIAL PLACE OF WOMEN AND MEN
and
HOSTILITY IN COUPLE IN RELATIONSHIPS

Segregated Schools

It seems I was happier in elementary school than I was in secondary school, because the secondary school I went to Lycée Toussaint **was** for boys only. I had excellent marks in elementary school. In secondary school my marks were not among the highest. When I was doing national exam in to go from grade 6 to grade 7, the teacher put two girls around me. He knew that the girls were a little bit weak in their courses. He put them beside me so that they can copy if need be. I was so happy and felt so proud about myself when the teacher did that, for although I was in the same classes with them for sometime, I never get that close to them, did not even think that I could ever get that close to them. The teacher guesses that that would make me happy. He was so right.

The point is that in such atmosphere there is no way you are going to become a violent partner in relationships with women. You would have already lived close by women who are not your sisters or your cousins. You would have already developed a certain ability to interact effectively with them. You would have already known them.

It the previous two chapter it is said again and again that lack of history in relationships with women is latent in most cases of violence in couples in relationships. When both partners in couples in relationships have been in schools, which are not segregated, they would already have a kind of vicarious history in the matter. So the potential for violence in their relationships is very low.

In the radio show called Rhona, the host almost always asked if they have sisters or brothers when a called and inquire about how to meet women or men. She is saying that if it's difficult for them to meet the opposite partners, to be in relationships with them, there is a lack of history with the opposite sex. I am saying that it is a cause for violence in couples in relationships.

In secondary school it was only men for me, so the only thing we did was fighting. I was not really doing the fighting, but sure was the object of violence from bullies.

Later in life, when my friends talk about fight they had with their girlfriends, it was as if they were talking about fight with other men. So when I was telling them about fight with my girlfriend it was as if I was talking about fight with other men. It was as if I was still in secondary school where all the students were men. So, in the relationships, when there is a fight, it's more likely that my friends and I we forget that she is the women we love. All that happened because we have been in segregated school.

Partly, I stopped to go to a university because I was annoyed by the sexual advances from professors (male and female) and students- male and male) toward me. Some other time I might have not paid attention to it that much. However, Just before I went to that university, I was moving from houses to houses, running away from other males who were bugging me with there homosexuality. It is why my reaction to what I encountered at the university was a little bit extreme.

While tutoring this student, he kept suggesting that I should have homosexual relation with him. He said it would be practical teaching. The problem is I am heterosexual. The problem is he was only 18 years old at that time. The problem is I was supposed to pass to him what I know about a foreign language he was learning, but I was not supposed to have something to do with his body, the physical part of his self. The problem is he was only in grade 12.

Even if we want it or not, non-segregated schools have something to do with what I call some kind of social degeneration. Educators must spend more of their times elaborating on the subject in order to come up with a course with content to prevent this kind of social degeneration created or amplified in non-segregated school. But, non-segregated school should not be stopped because of that, for the result would be worse for us, there would be more violence in men /women relationships.

Patriarchal Society

There have been a few women occupying the position of chief of state in the world and across human history. I am thinking of Indira Ghandi of India, Margaret Thatcher of England, B. Butho of Pakistan. Imagine a world of 190 countries trying to eliminate women will to decide for themselves what is good for themselves, it is violence against them, nor does it set the tone for respect toward them. I can scarcely count 3 chiefs of state across human history who were women. Do we need to demonstrate that patriarchal society (all by men and for men) has existed, exists, and probably will exist in the future? One cannot argue that the state of things is that way because women do not like being chief of state, for there is no study that have shown so. Then, there are writing on that men want to keep women under control, because when they get free they will perform better than the men will. At the beginning of human history some ideas like that were floating around the fear of women overpowering men with their wit.

Women at the House

It is to assume that at the beginning of life, women staid in the hole in the mountain used as houses while men go outside hunting It was like that because of the necessity of the starting life time. In modern societies this state of affairs is bit different, for there is enough time for some learning to have taken place. Yesterday February 20, 2005, subject of discussion on television of radio Canada was "Should the federal government of Canada create and manage Day Care or should money be given to couples and let them to decide for themselves how they're going to take care of their kids and working at the same time?"

By the time the decision is made, the book or Relations Amoureuses will not be published yet. I have two other books: *The Soul Exposed*, *Kickitwell Or Else*, which haven't been published yet. The second is written and rewritten since 1993. All that to say that my skill at publishing my work are very poor if not to say inexistent or I just met the brick wall trying to publish (African descent and being born in francophone society, may be). Anyway, my position on the choice between the government Day Care and families Day Care, is I would pick the latter without a doubt, for it's clear that government efficiency in running business is as poor as my skills in publishing. That's why there are Crown Corporations and business in some ex-communists countries which had collapsed and that in some other communists countries they made a "retour en douceur" to market economy.

The point is that the Day Care initiative of the government shows that in 2005 women are still forced to stay at the house if they have kids for not having enough money to pay Day Care and that this situation leaves us the sense of women as being inferior comparatively to men, diminishes them, is violence against them, and again sets the tone for violence against them in relationships.

To the economical violence created by that women are forced to stay at the house and violence against them in relationships are the direct result of the patriarchal society. For some men the place of women is at the house. We can take the example of Barbara. She said to me that she has a diploma in architecture. They are living in the same small house that I share with them, meaning that they are not rich. At the same time they have two kids. Still Barbara is not working outside. I lived in the same house for about 6 years. I conclude that it is because her husband Todd prefer the situation that way, that he likes his woman at the house taking care of kids. It would never be in the advantage of Barbara to want to stay at the house. That's why she went to school and studied architecture.

One of my girlfriends had a friend named Debbie. When I just met her she was working for a company, which was selling high-tech devices (Internet services, cellular phone, etc.). As soon as she gets married, she stopped working, had kids. She said that her husband, who was himself free lance accountant, doesn't want her working outside. It is not clear if men notice it, or even if women themselves notice it, but it is violence against women, for the situation in most cases (if we exclude individual choices) will prevent them from fulfilling their lives as HBBs. One of the conditions for that is working at something, trying to achieve a goal fulfill their potential as HBBs which most of the time takes them out of the house. AT all cases they should be free to choose to work at the house or working outside.

Women at Work

At work, the state of affairs is not different either. Women do the same amount of work than men and get paid less for it. The bulk of the women do menial work, secretarial work. So they are considered as being inferior to men. It is potential for violence against them in relationships with men.

At the same time women would loose there by trying to emulate, that would mean they are trying to be like men. That is the worst mistake that could ever be. They would not even really know who they are like and it is a capital sin not trying to be like oneself (In an interview I saw the black kids saying that the white kids are eating sirloin, driving nice car, again they are committing the grossest mistake by trying to be like the white kids, consequently by not trying to be themselves .

Crime against Women

Picton was a pig farmer in Coquitlam, suburb of Vancouver, British Columbia. Police found remains of around 50 women bodies buried in his farm. The estimation of the number of women prostitute he has killed is in the hundred (So much evidences why a trial, it seems like a charade to me). Another serial killer in United States of America this time is named the Green River killer. He has killed a number of prostitute women similar to the number Picton has killed. They both claimed that they did it because they thought they could get away with it. They thought like that because those women are not well seen by the rest of the rest of us, by society.

The point is that part of male mentality affects couples in relationships enormously. In other words, part of violence in couples in relationships is direct result of social stigma toward women. If there weren't this social negative tag on prostitute, those women in United States and in Canada would not be dead before they have lived their lives. They social stigma may be not easy to come by with, not easy to erase, but if prostitution was legal in those countries, it is likely that those women would not be dead before their time, in one hand. In the other, it would have a better effect on couples in relationships.

There even is a dissonance theory according to which the way we treat a person would affect our liking of that person. The Picton and Green River killer "effect" verify the theory.

The essence of the book is to diminish the gap between men and women, not to divide them. But reality may be harshed, violence in couples in relationships is only the extreme form of social conditions of women, the extreme form of how women is seen by society in general, an inferior being.

There will be a time when all schools will be non-segregated, when all societies will be matriarchal and patriarchal, social regard toward men and women will be balanced so much so that conditions of women at work, at the house, will be all well, when there will be no crime against women, so much so that couple's relationships will be perfect harmony (Europe was an equality society once). However our imagined world is perfect but not possible. Nonetheless, one more reason to keep our attention on these subjects in order to make "la vie à deux" something we crave, something that promote life, creativity in order to ameliorate human life on earth.

I met so many men in Vancouver. I could not develop a friendships with them, not because it is not something I would like, not because I don't think it's something important in life, but because of their homosexuality. Something is socially wrong. When some men are homosexual that will do no wrong to anybody. But it is the quantities of them that worries me (I know the heterosexuals are there otherwise there would not homosexual bashing). Laura Bush reminded me of that in an interview with Barbara Walter when she said that she will pay more attention to boys, for our attention, nowadays, is on girls, we are more focused on girls, while the boys seem to be left aside, left to themselves. So it is another problem in the horizon, another social imbalance started to be created. We have to hurry in preventing it from happening. Otherwise we are in for a shock, for another social arrangement that will have a very negative impact in couples in relationships.

IV

MISCELLANEOUS ITEMS

Criminal Individuals and Violence in Couples in Relationships

Some individuals are criminals. Wouldn't it be nice if there was no criminal among HBBs? There wouldn't be no fear against crime against oneself, no jail, no police, no war. That would be a peaceful life forever. We would be busy in creativity, busy ameliorating the conditions of our lives. So our imaginative life without crime wouldn't be necessarily boring as it appears.

Unfortunately, life on Earth now is not like that. There are wars, organized crime, serial killers, and individuals committing all sorts of crimes every day. To witness that one only has to open a newspaper, or listen to radio or watch TV at news hours. This week (Today is March 8, 2005) it was reported that a married man had three lives: one at work, one with his family (wife and kids), and the other one with young girls from 2 to 14 that he kidnapped on the street or somewhere and rapes and killed. He was cut on the spot and sent to jail. His wife explained that he spent much of his time in the computer, and that he used to get violent with her, that he used to beat her.

The one girl he did not rape and kill said that his father told her if she was accosted with gun or knife pointed at her by a stranger if it's outside she should scream, for he would kill her anyway after he rapes her, that if it was inside, that would be the call of the girl to run. So that what she did, and the criminal run away. It was outside, she yelled for help.

What I am trying to say is that it is up to partners in relationships to make sure that the other partner is not a criminal, doesn't have a criminal character or background or a criminal reccord. Some HBBs may change, that's why I call them HBBs (human being becoming) anyway. However, if your partner corresponds to the one we've just described, your relationships are in jeopardy, there may be violence in your relationships, even you yourself is in great danger. In other words, in relationships, you must be sure you are not dealing with a criminal (Forget about the thrill for the bad boy appetite, it is sure to get you in tombstone very quickly, unless you are one of those philosophers who says that life is very short, die now or later does not matter.

I do not want really to go into the crime circumstances in order not to justify them, but crime is when HBBs are miserable, misery caused by poverty, ignorance, when there is a group of HBBs of different races living close by, when there is inner conflict in HBBs, especially when parents stay steadfast with the idea that their kids should be like them, their kids cannot develop their own individuality. From crime, we could go to organized crime. We would be out of topic, out of what I call domestic violence.

Stress and Violence in Couples in Relationships

It is the name given to a common psychological reality. It's like a HBB cannot be without having to deal with stress almost all along the continuum of his life span. In other words any kind of life you are living, you will have to cross stressful situations, any kind of activity you are doing, you will have some stressful moments in it. Stress kind of defines us.

The same goes for couples in relationships.

There is an element of unknown in a stressful situation. We are going to ask for a raise in our job, we don't know how our boss will react, we are stressful, or we become unusually tense. So there is also an element of tension in stress (tension is the name of stress in French). When we are about to talk to a group of HBBs, our heart rate rises; we may feel suet in our hands. All that indicates that we are stressful.

Stress is the most faithful companion I have in my life. When I just arrived in Vancouver, I was a teacher on call in many school districts in smaller cities around Vancouver. In one School district there are many schools I had to go to. In a school, I had about 5 classes a day, meaning 5 different groups of about 25 students I didn't know at all. So the stressful situation started at 5 in the morning when they call me to go to new school district, to a new school. I had to find it in map and drove to arrive on time, which were usually 8 am. The most stressful in it was at the beginning dealing with the new classes, because everything was new to me. After a while I memorized a bit, it became less stressful.

One thing I was going to forget to mention about the break-up with Georgette was the stress factor. I did not consider it as a factor at that time unknowingly. Now I figure it out for at the same time I was living with her I was going to many colleges, I was a student. I had many classes everyday including Saturday. I had to study and pass the exams. It was, indeed, a situation too stressful to promote "la vie à deux" avec Georgette and, it explains my violent behaviour in regard to her plus my self-inadequacies as suggested above.

The importance of the management of your stress may not be clear to you, but under stress, we will do things we would never do in a normal situation. In a stressful situation we may forget our own name. This lady and I had to meet because she was doing a work for me. She used to flirt with me at her place in the presence of her husband. At that time her parents were visiting her from France. That day she decided to meet me in her house before the arrival of her parents who were visiting the city and her husband who were still at work. I met her in the back of her house, but she forgot her keys at work. We had to wait for her parents and her husband before we can get into the house. She was under a tremendous amount of stress caused by the idea of her marriage and having an intimate relation with me.

(I have read in a psychology book of a person who forgot his own name for 20 minutes after an exam she passes with the best mark. It's like she was totally someone else during the exam.)

In a small book I wrote and called *Kickitwell or Else*, there is a part on stress. There even is a stress curve, which allows seeing at a glance the effective amount stress in someone's life and the distress followed by other diseases that can occur when we go beyond the threshold of the effective amount of stress. You can consult the book in order to use the knowledge on stress. It may help to avoid pitfalls in your relationships.

Stress is when we are engaged in an activity or about to engage in an activity but we don't know if we have enough background to do well, if we are well equipped enough to do well, if we are going to be able to cope with the activity. Among all activities relationships are the most stressful, for two HBBs of different background are joined together mentally at least. You ask yourself if you are going to be able to continue to please the other person. If you are married, you're wondering about what you will do to take care of your wife and children, if you are laid off your work, without a job. Those questions are enough to put you in a frenzy mood, which may change the sweetest person into a beast.

Wrong Assumption, Beliefs, Values and Violence in Couples in Relationships

Assumption

When I went to that woman's place and saw a man inside, I became mad immediately. I had the key of the door, tried to use it to go inside. Her and the man blocked the door with their bodies first then locked it. I was still mad; broke the glace window and passed through it to go inside. I've never met him before, but he and the woman were co-workers. Many wrong assumptions have contributed to cause the violent situation. She assumed that I would not go to her place that time. She assumed that if I tried to open the door and found that they would not let me in, I would go back to where I came from. They assumed that I was not a violent person so that I would not become violent if saw them together.

When I first met her, I was going out a lot, told something about going out with many women at a time, suggesting that she can do the same also. The violent incident happened 6 years later. When I told it to her she said no squarely, I accepted it and forgot about the unusual proposition. It only quite later after the incident I remember that she was behaving with me and her girlfriends in way that suggested that I should sleep with them. At that time I realized what was going on, that she was putting the unusual proposition of 6 years ago in application assuming that I would remember and made the connections with the present situation. She assumed wrongly for I had totally forgotten about it then. That was the biggest factor in the causality of the violent incident.

In my side I assumed that she was having an affair with the married man I saw inside of her apartment, but he could have been a neighborhood who came to talk to her about an event in the neighbour, or somebody who were trying to sell her a vacuum cleaner, for example.

Beliefs

A belief is the way you think things happen, they way you think they are done, your theories on life events.

The way you see it is that the belief becomes an attitude, the attitude itself becomes a motivation in the right context. At the level of motivation we are very close to action. It should be the road beliefs follow to manifest themselves in our life. Then, as we have seen, they do not need our will. Or we could say the fact that we believe means that we will.

It is why in life it is always a good thing to do to find out who we really are, a good thing to pay attention to our selves (instead of always watching TV, comparing ourselves to others, or listening to friends, or others). By listening to ourselves we may know what's wrong in our lives and do the necessary to correct it. The prompt is not always obvious. Sometimes we may have to go through a lot of steps before we reach it. Sometimes we may have to do a lot of diggings before we find what is wrong with us.

In other words beliefs are usually unconscious, and even may be genetic (If fear can be genetic, so can be beliefs). There are a lot of "bs" they told us since we came to life until we are able to think for ourselves. I did not say until we are adult, because adults also may not be in position to think for themselves (According to some psychological theories genes do not determine our lives).

If a man believes that he has to show to his woman that he is strong to be loved by her for his strength, that belief may bring violence into the relationships, for many reasons. The first one is that the object of the believe is unreal. A lot of women do not think like that. If the woman in the relationships do not think like that, there is a major background for miscommunication, misunderstanding in the relationships. They bound to bring quarrels. From the quarrels there may be some frustration, non-satisfaction and violence.

If a HBB believes that "life is a burden", that, also, may bring violence to the relationships. It means that we have to struggle, we have to suffer, and we have to wear the cross. To fulfill the belief both members of the relationships may resort to violence. To all practical ends, this belief is a justification of war.

Values

Mike was living in the same house than me. He was a bisexual. When he moved in the house, her girlfriend broke up with him. He left the house in which he was living with her and moved in where I was living a house in which there were most of the time 7 bodies sharing it. After the woman broke up with Mike, he was suffering a little bit. Before he moved in he might not think that I was heterosexual. Anyway, he showed me one letter he received from the ex-girlfriend in which she said to him that Mike and her might have different values. She was so right, I wander if she knew that Mike was a bisexual.

Nevertheless, the incident is like a hands on practice of how values interplay in relationships, the role they play in relationships. In regard to Mike and his girlfriend, they have only caused the break-up. In other cases, it could have been different, in other cases the results could have been violence in couples in relationships. In their case the break-up was a way to avoid violence. In other case it could have been different. Mike valued his homosexuality, not how beautiful and understanding she was.

In psychology they talk about critical component of value. It seems to have a cost (fear of both success and failure, amount of effort to succeed, and lost of opportunities for choosing one course of action than another). In this context it is applied to a goal. It could be applied to relationships also, for each one of the two members of the relationships has values, even if they are at a conscious level or not. Then, it is important to find out what our values are in order for them not to trigger negative atmosphere in our relationships, in order for them not to make you hit your girlfriend because you are not valuing her (you may be a matcho man, a homosexual, etc.) It could be the other way around too, meaning, the woman may well be the one who is not valuing the man.

I do not know if Carla Omolka pushed Paul Bernado to rape young girls and killed them, or if the violence came from Bernado himself. To put it differently I do not know which one has violent temper in the relationships, nor if it is both of them who were violent persons. What I am trying to say is that women can be the violent one in the relationships too, and that the subject is of utmost importance, for we are not talking only about member of a relationships always quarrelling, or one member of a relationships hitting the other. We are also saying that unchecked values may bring one member of the relationships to kill the other. How many times we hear of those stories in the news.

It is happened from time to time. In the news recently it was question of two men killing their girlfriends (something bizarre, a father killed his daughter, because she was seeing a guy of another race). Nowadays the famous case is Scott Peterson in jail for killing his wife, before it was OJ Simpson who was accused of killing his wife and her lover. According to these news it is a common fact of life. What I want to draw attention to is that violence in couples is more common than that, than what is reported in the news, that most of the violence in relationships are not reported, and that women are for the big part the victims, being physically smaller than men.

Irrational Valuation and Violence in Couples in Relationships

The Hero

Most of the time the hero will want to protect his women. Will play the father figure as far as she is concerned and even as far as everybody else is concerned. The hero is the antagonist of the criminal, the bad person. So it is not in that sense I see him as potential for violence in a relationships. I see him that way because of his strength. Like the lion that picked-up Roy, almost killed him by doing so. The lion had no intention to hurt Roy.

Most of the time the hero is craved of adulations from others. In that sense he is wrong, takes him away from himself. His strength is a wrong one, he is dangerous, can make things worse even with the intention of making things right.

The Bad Boy

It's not very easy to understand why they are like that but some women like bad boys. Psychologists would say that those women who like bad boys are sado-masochistic or had sexual traumas in chilhood, or that they were brought up in a violent atmosphere. The worst of it all is that boys and men pick up the trend (women like bad boys) and try to be bad in order to attract these women. The way wrap musicians dress already indicates that they are bad boys. Michael Jackson sang a sung with title "I am bad". He likes to be a bad boy so much that it is likely why he is in court now accused of abusing children. "I am bad" is the title of one of his songs.

In this context, some men will be violent with women in other to show to them that they are bad boys, or they have some of it in them. And as it is already writtenrd in this book, we play with negative feeling at our own risk, our own expense, for after the negative feelings started, no one knows where it is going to stop. The negative feeling that has started by the love of bad boys may end in violence and death.

Negative/Positive Feelings and Violence in Couple in Relationships

Negative Feelings

MISOGYNOUS MEN

How does a man do to be a woman hater? Does it come from an exaggerated sense of masculinity? A society with accentuation on masculinity? Is it because of a society with too many labels, too many dividers, too many walls or a society about to become too masculine (I was going to say about to become astray)? This kind of men reminds us of the one who killed the women at the University of Montreal. It is the extreme form of the women hater, but it is clear that there is some of it too in violence in couples in relationships. Most of the time we are like that without even noticing it.

JEALOUSY

I myself was a very jealous person when I was younger. It probably originated in that mother who left this world when I was between 5 and 6 years old. Our father had some other women and some other children. I was very jealous of the other children because of the tenderness with which their mothers treated them, what I did not have. Because of that, also, I became very solitary, very shy.

A little bit of jealousy in relationships lets the other partner know that there is love in the relationships according to some psychologists. Again it is a slippery slope, for it can become a big deal in a iota of time, and when it becomes that way, watch out.

That is to say egocentric jealousy is only destructive.

Positive Feelings

In the book *How to Get from Where you Are to Where you Want to Be*, Sheri Hubert the author wrote that she had affection for an old man and then she felt like hitting him. It was the repressed feelings of affection that brought the emotion of violence in her.

The same psychological phenomenon has already been observed in chapter 3 of this book with title "The function of sexual frustration in violence in relationships", fundamental argument anyway, in which chapter it is argued that sexual frustration is one of the causes of violence in couple in relationships. In other words with Cheri the phenomenon can be seen on an emotional (some author distinguishes emotion and feelings; here they are used as synonym) angle, in this book it is treated on a sexuality angle. However, I find it important enough to develop it a little bit more.

REPRESSED POSITIVE FEELINGS AND VIOLENCE

Who knows how many crimes have been committed with it at the root cause without ever coming on the surface of our consciousness, how many HBBs are in psychiatric Hospitals after having been diagnostized as schizophrenic, but who in reality are just suffering from repressed positive feelings?

Yesterday Tuesday, May 3, 2005, in a meeting about voting in the next Provincial Election, a girl came a little bit late and sat by me. Then, she asked me for a pen. I had an extra pen I gave it to her with the intention of not taking it back. But I expected that after the training session she was going to think of me and at that moment I was going to ask her if she could go and have a coffee with me. She had stimulated my appetite, or it takes very little to stimulate my appetite at these times, being in a long sexual abstinence and not being sick in bed.

After the session, she left the pen on the table and left. She didn't do anything wrong by sitting by me. For there weren't to many empty chairs left, however I felt frustrated.

The school where I was going to work on Election Day was dictated to me on the phone. I felt there was something wrong about the explanation given to me as to how to find the school. After the meeting I went and verified that it was really wrong, that the school was at 15 minutes walk away from where I thought it would be at first. However, near the school I had the need to pee. A few blocks from there I finished by finding a garage where I can pee, but I had to stand a bit inside the garage to do it trough a hole in the wall of the garage. There was a car in it, I was standing very close to it, if they owner of the place saw me, I would be in very big trouble, thinking that I was about to steal his car and call the police.

All in all, the above paragraph is saying that sexual frustration was the cause of my violent behaviour, peeing in the garage of someone else.

SEXUAL RESTRICTIONS/INTERDICTIONS AND SEXUAL TABOOS

Speaking of repressed positive feelings, one cannot prevent oneself from thinking of sexual taboos in society in general and especially sexual taboos and the church.

Where do sexual taboos come from? In society-humanist pulsion takes over- in general it must be instinctive, for sexuality create a very positive feeling in us. Some human beings are addicted to sex, or, we should rather have said that sex can be, is very addictive. Children and even adolescents cannot have sex without seriously damaging their psychological make-up. There are all sorts of small sexual diseases, all sorts of big sexual diseases. Some of them are not completely curable. It is probably why we have sexual taboos, a way for different species to survive, our way for our species to survive. Animals do not have sexual taboos, or none that we know of. They must be going at it wildly, but they do not destroy themselves with it, instinctively again.

SEXUAL RESTRICTIONS/INTERDICTIONS AND TABOOS IN CHURCH

When I was adolescent, I used to get up at 3 AM to wash in a little river passing behind my parents' place, to walk for about 30 minutes to go to the 4 AM Mass in "Saint Rosaire" the name of a church in a suburb of Port-au-Prince called Croix-des-Bouquets. Nowadays, I can not even remember the last time I went to a church; I do not do such thing any longer. I am no longer such a religious person. However, church was useful to humanity on many aspects, especially around the beginning of our lives on earth. That where literacy has started.

Then, humanity has grown up in the sense that our actual needs are not quite the same as they were before. But it seems that the mentality in the churches does not change, especially in catholic religion where women can not be priest, where priest cannot be married, cannot have sexual relation, where abortion is not accepted, no matter in which circumstances it happened, no matter how dangerous the pregnancy can be for the woman if it continues, etc, etc. Men and women cannot have sexual relation before they get married.

All in all there are a lot of restrictions/interdictions around sexuality in churches. It becomes a taboo. They generate illnesses in some HBBs, opposite reaction in some others who become addicted to sex, sex slave etc.

So, the church, which was so useful at the beginning of humanity, turns out to be not so useful anymore and can even be an handicap in the sense that it prevent some of us to be who we can be, from being able to use all our potentials, from being able to use as many of our possibilities as possible, imprisoned in religious restrictions/interdictions and taboos. And, restriction on the body is to all-practical ends restriction on the soul and spirit, because of the closeness or we could say, <u>because of the inseparability between the body, the soul, and the spirit</u> (In some psychological theories it says the spirit has to be differentiated from the soul) The restriction is cause for violence in relationships.

PART II

SMOOTH RELATIONSHIPS

INNER RELATEDNESS FOR SMOOTH RELATIONSHIPS

Anger Management

The book is called *The Magic of Rapport*. In it there is this part where they give advice on how to deal with an angry or hostile person. In relationships the situation may be not as extreme as suggested below. Most of the time members of a couple only argue. However, will help to calm down an angry or hostile partner:

Disarming Verbal Anger and Hostility

Know that whenever someone attacks you, your idea or something with which you are associated, the issue to deal with is not the content of the attack but rather the attacker's anger. Know that in most instances ,defensiveness is a radical error, because it can readily be taken by the other person as a counter attack and as such serves only to increase the level of anger and hostility.

All in all, I learned that when anger change into rage it is no longer a "normal" emotion, it becomes a selfish feeling where one individual is totally unconcerned about others.

Expression of Feelings

In general and in most societies of the world expression of feelings is more or less accepted from women, but mot from men. So most of the times the males are bottled up, not having learned how to let their feelings out, except in outrageous actions. A big part of violence in relationships is the result of that kind of situation.

The lost of emotional expressivities is not only conducive to violence in couple in relationships, but is also conducive to death. After a long period of time without being able to express ourselves emotionally, we loose the natural ability of having feelings. At that point we are dying or dead.

However, the other extreme of the emotional continuum is as negative, without being able to short down the emotional surplus will bring us mental sicknesses such as depression or even illnesses requiring psychiatric intervention.

Meditation for Better Relations

Meditation is the easiest way to relate to yourself. It can be done any time of the day at home or at work, in a crowd or alone. The person doing meditation in a crowd would have to have experience in meditation or in a very particular situation as a group kidnapping for in it you would have lot of time to meditate or to withdraw from the group mentally and talk to yourself in order to find your way out of the kidnapping alive. Fortunately you will not meditate in such harsh situation. On the contrary you are going to meditate to take your relationships with your partner to a higher level so that both of you can be happy and grow together.

It would be better if both of you could meditate together, but if it is not possible, it will not be the sea to drink the schedule will be established by you, twice a week, or 3 times a week. You sit comfortably on a sofa trying to relax for part of the time (relaxation techniques are almost everywhere, in most of the books written on earth). So, you relax and keep in mind the one question for the session that you are looking an answer for. In our case it is how to make the relationships with your partner work better?

There are physical tension and psychic tension: (good for creation) when we are about to meet an important person, waiting for an important decision etc. To get rid of physical tension, you relax. To appease psychic tension, you meditate.

Talk to Yourself

It is a technique I use very frequently for it is easy to use. You just need paper and pencil or pen. For it, also, you can be at home or at work, in a group or singly. You write down questions and wait for answers that you write down equally. If there are a lot of issues in your mind, you may be drag from one end of a spectrum to the other, if there are unusual events happening in the world at the same time you are talking to yourself, you may be dragged from one end of the spectrum to the other. To stay focused you keep asking the same question until you have the answer.

Sometimes, you may have answers, as you are about to write down the questions. So it is a fast process, be alert and keep the pace with it.

At the same time you are talking to yourself, try to be aware of everything that is happening around you. Some of it may be clue to the answer of the question you are asking.

Stay away from negative feelings as much as you can, from ideas that are not what you are looking for at this particular moment when you are trying to find ideas on how to develop satisfying and durable relationships. Keep all ideas that create negative feelings at bay for the moments and focused on the task at hand.

DPs in Good Interaction

DPs are what I call direct perceptions and what you called dreams in your day to day life. As it is said in the first part of the book everyone has them, even if we do not all notice it. To be aware of our dreams, we have to have a firm decision to know about them. That is why it is good also to do incubation which is to have a sheet of paper on which you write down the question of which you need an answer. Sometimes just the question will be enough, some other times it makes things easier if you start answering the question yourself before waiting for dream on it.

In our case we are trying to use our dreams to make our relationships better. Incubation will be on the issues of the relationships in couple. In the first part of the books we have dealt with some of the negative issues, but you may have issues more particular to your relation.

In other words our incubation is on how to keep violence out of the relationships. Is it something wrong I am doing? What am I doing wrong that may trigger violence in my relationships? You go on like that until you have no more questions. The sheet of paper is near where you sleep if you want to wake up at night to write the dream which will be on the questions that you have asked, even if it is not apparent to you at first. So you write down anything, small or big, short or long.

If you do not want to wake up immediately after the dream to write it down, you can choose to write first time in the morning. Later you may forget it. Also, you do not want to go to walk while being obsessed by your dreams you want to keep but did not have enough time to write down. So if you do not wake up immediately to write it down, or if you do not write down first thing in the morning you may forget it.

Your incubation may also be to find the potential issues of the relationships related to violence. In other words, the incubation may be on the questions instead of the answers.

Some of the dream observers suggest that we recreate the pass by focusing on our dream meanings related to us only. So you may forget about dream interpretation totally, or you may do it with a universal perspective.

Effective Communication Means

The title of this sub chapter is inspired by another subchapter in the first part of the book, that is "ritualization of ambivalence". As we have seen, the mild negative feelings involved in it may skid to strong negative feelings when triggered by any event, then it may have the opposite effects than the ones expected which were mainly bringing partners closer, keep excitement alive in the relations). Instead of that "ritualization of ambivalence"(members of couple who quarrel often to spice it up) may cause violence.

The alternatives to "ritualization of ambivalence is exactly the object of this chapter. So they are: "meditation for better relations", "self-talk", "DPs in good interaction" Effective Communication Means and "expression of love".

Keeping excitement in relationships is not always necessary. That is to say that it is not the only way to make it last, to keep it smooth, without to big bumps. The importance attached to the relationships is also a way to make it last, keep it more or less levelled down. In different words, unless you change partners regularly, it may be less easy to keep the excitement upbeat, which is not necessary either. Something else plays the same function as excitement, something easier to come by with, easier to keep, that is the importance of the relationships for you, how valuable it is for you.

Another ineffective communication means in "la vie à deux"that I have observed is the use of metaphor. It may be efficient after a certain time in relationships, but not at the beginning.

Amorous partners' behaviuor at the beginning of the association is not what it could be. Their behaviour is a little bit clumsy. Not because they are young or anything like that, but because it is the beginning of the liaison, a lot of emotions are involved. At this stage the relationships is like a human baby born a few days ago, unable to stand on his own and walk. That's why we make blunders when we've just met our beloved.

Then, you add to that metaphor, symbolization, you are in for trouble. So, instead of that, you better say what you mean and mean what you say to your partner at the beginning of the love association.

Expression of Love

Feelings (or emotions) are not easy to express. If all feelings were positive, it would probably be easier to express them. Because they are not always positive they are blocked in our psyche. An emotion, as the name indicate (motion) is something passing, we do not really know what they are for never having enough time to study them. Most of the time they past as quickly as they arrive.

They are not substantial, although they may start by a substantial event as touching.

The expression of love is a particular case for it is a positive expression, expressing it should be like eating a cake. On the contrary, for some of us it is the most difficult thing to do. Most of the time we are not sure if we love the person or not. When we do love her, we are not certain that she loves us as well, even if she says so because of the unsubstantial nature of love.

Then in some society, it's like it is not well seen when a man uses loving expressions to address his fiancée or his wife. In the first days of my going-out-with-Debbie, once I used the word darling to address her. She was so mad because of that. I felt if she had something in her hands she would hit me with it. According to her it was making a blunder on my part, even though I said that because I felt close to her.

So, the potential for violence is prevalent in such society, for feelings are not only naturally difficult to deal with, difficult to express, to identify but also HBBs are encouraged to repress them. They will have, then, a tendency to use behaviour, their hands, to express their feelings.

That's it I am going to say it. Difficult or not, the expression of love (or similar expression such as dear, sweetie, baby, honey, dear, dearest, sugar, beloved, precious, pet, babe, etc, using them and meaning them) in relationships will do much more than getting partners closer, it will, also, make the relationships smoother. These partners will have relationships without the avoidable quarrels, hurts, and definitely not violence. When days of lovers are sprinkled with these words, they are sure to be without feelings that could degenerated in violence. Positive emotions eliminate negative ones most of the time.

Most of the time couples love each other in relationships, but it still doesn't go well. The bumps are so hard that if one partner does not withdraw from the association, there will be a victim. Behind the difficulty is a split psyche. Inner relatedness (or communication between conscious and unconscious part of the self for better communication with partner) is always the best tool to use to overcome that situation.

In his book *Making Contact* (to overcome shyness, making new relationships and keeping those you already have), Arthur C. Wosner says that "deterioration of contact in marriage is in my view the most common marital problem, occurring more often than incidences of adultery, physical brutality, financial mismanagement and sexual incompability combined......." Although it may appear to you to be a discourse very different than the one in Relation Amoureuse, but in reality it is not. Physical brutality is the subject developed most in the first part of Relation Amoureuse. Sexual incompability is similar to the chapter of Sexual Frustration ...... in first part Relation Amoureuse.

All in all, in Relation Amoureuse, there is a consideration oriented more toward an inner explanation than it is in some other books in psychology. However, in *Making Contact* Arthur made a good summarization of couples' issues.

VI

ROMANTIC LOVE
and
ITS POSITIVE EFFECTS ON COUPLES

Romantic Love and Health

When I am in love (passionate love), I tend to have healthier attitude, healthier behaviour. First of all we need nothing. There is a saying in French that illustrates the idea: "l'amour et l'eau froide" love and cold water meaning that it is all that lovers need to live. Men in love become more themselves, more courageous. Women in love become more languorous more feminine, more themselves also. We tend to pay more attention to other HBBs in difficulty we meet in the street. If a couple of lovers meet a blind HBBs, one or both them will offer the person a hand, offer to show him/her the way.

Second, it's like all our neurosis are vanished and gone, especially about love and sexuality. We become innocent like children, without any reluctance to show our love for each other in the presence of other HBBs. Love cures all. No guilt, no shame, sexual body totally accepted, no mental hang-ups.

Love is a bundle of positive emotions as it is written in the first chapter of the book (but emotion always implies action and thoughts in causal and circular relation). When we add intensity and passion to it as in romantic love, the composite turns out to be the most efficient tool lovers can create for themselves, the most magnificent feeling that can be, and the most magnificent medicine that can be. That's how love does its "miracles", why we say it cures all.

I felt in love with Georgette, I took more courses in colleges than usual, didn't even have time to be with her. It was when I had the best marks for all the courses I had ever taken. I did not know how to manage my life at the time; did not make the best of what was happening to me. If I did, who knows what I would be doing now, who knows how many of my goals I would already be enjoying, how many HBBs I would have helped in the process?

Of course mental health means body health and that the two together are prediction for healthy relationships. In such association, there can be quarrels and arguments, but only the manageable ones, the ones that can be controlled, the ones that will not tear the relation apart violently.

Some of you believe that we have to struggle in life(then there could be violence in relationships). However I do not believe so. Life is dynamic, there are ups and downs, struggle is not necessary.

Romantic Love and Creativity

Sometimes loves starts right away, it is love at first sight as you say (Is it not always that way deep down). It has happened to me with Linda who I met in club in Quebec City once. She was wearing a white dress, she was so nice looking, and I dance with her all night. She was with a group of friends in the club she went back to Montreal with them; I went back to Montreal alone as I went to Quebec. In Montreal the day after I was very upset in a good way by that I have danced for a long time the previous day. I could not take my mind from her during the whole day, the whole week until I met her again.

She came to my place, after she left, I still couldn't keep my mind off of her. I thought of her all the time. However, at that time I was still too young to care, did not have a plan to be in a stable connection with a woman yet. Linda and me drifted away from each other physically, but it was an intense love between us, therefore more than 20 years later she is still in my active mind.

Etiennette, the godmother that I have or had, was married with Job Joseph all the time I've known them. They are about the same height in the short size. They had Camita, Marguerita, Chantal, Marco, and Marcel, 5 children together. They only time Etiennette and Job were not together were when Etiennette had to be away in the capital to sell the products of their farms and buy what is needed in the area where they lives. Otherwise, Job and her were together everyday almost all the time. They woke up in the morning, at around 6 AM, went to work in their farm and came back home at 6 PM.

Etiennette and Job never fought, were never mad at each other as far as I know. I was at their house often. I didn't have a mother. Etiennette was like one to me.

So there was definitely romantic love between them.

Gerard Toussaint is a friend I met at secondary school. Since he met Mary, they were together everyday for some time at the beginning of the relationships. When I met Gerard, he was always talking about Mary in a frenetic way, and telling Me about the intensity of positive feelings she created in him after a few months in Canada he arranged to get Mary here too and they got married.

They are another example of romantic love, which may be defined as loving with intensity and passion. I feel that I would be with the person all the time. When I am not with him or her, I am worried. Other HBBs and other things even working are no longer meaningful to the romantic lover. She and the beloved are like the only two persons, the only thing existing on the planet.

To give a complete account of the love phenomenon, we must bring also a very important aspect of it, which is surrendering. It is such an essential part of love that according to some authors some men cannot love exactly because it is difficult for them to surrender. However, for love to endure, according to these love observers, surrendering must be reciprocal, intermittent. Men unable to love because they do not want to surrender may not know about the reciprocal aspect of the surrendering.

Then there is that men are supposed to be strong, surrendering for these men would be a weakness, we have already discussed this aspect of love above. So it is not easy for men to love especially in the modern Western world.

In his book *Motivation/Theories and Principles,* Robert C. Beck cites Davis Who proposed in 1985 that liking (friendships) consists of enjoyment, mutual assistance, spontaneity, acceptance, trust, understanding and confidence; that love consists of all the elements of liking plus the elements of passion, sexual desire, exclusiveness and caring (surrendering). The proposition of Davis on love is more like romantic love to me. Anyway that's what I mean by romantic love.

Romantic love exists since the night of time everywhere on the planet in almost all countries between HBBs with all backgrounds. However, it is more apparent in HBBs in Hollywood, not only in like Warren Beatty and Frank Sinatra, but also in persons like Britney, Donald Trump or Elizabeth Taylor despite their numerous marriages. As a matter of fact, the numerous marriages are more the sign of HBBs looking for partner with whom to be in romantic love, than married couples who stay together and are miserable. Then, they are among the most successful HBBs in the world. It is possible to conclude that there is a link between romantic love and their successful endeavors, therefore between romantic love and creativity.

The same way it is likely that among HBBs, who are single, some of them are romantic lovers. In other words, they are singles because they are romantic lovers not being able to find a partner who matches their romantic aspirations, romantic partners becoming a rare commodity, especially in the 21 century in developed countries.

Although, at the same time, scientific and technological development continuing its ascending curve, make it possible for men and women to be able to meet each other with less difficulty than it was in the past. There is, the internet match makers with the internet chat rooms, "some especially designed for the young and lonely, for busy professional, for widows and widowers, for Asian, Black, or alternative, via phone or online, with videos introduction and personality tests, pre-screened, and qualified with phone and essay included" (Bruce Brander). There is even mail order bride, though not groom from Russia, Ukraine and the Philippines. I myself, I look for women wherever I can meet them, meaning according to my activities, in the street, in libraries, and so on.

Nowadays, there is Poppy in TV I would like to meet her. I have sent her a letter and have no answer from her. She may be "married with children". Right? Or Natalie in miss universe I would like to meet. You don't even know how to get in touch with her yet. Plus she, also, may be "married with children".

When you are heterosexual and spend 7 years without ever touching a woman, you have strange love and sexual feelings sometimes.

I have a group of women with whom I have psychic experience. There are some celebrities in it (we'll do better not go there), it can be shocking to you the reader to find out who they are: a Queen, Jessica(s), Avril, etc., and they haven't been picked by me, they just show themselves to my psychic parties, and some of them are married. When I told them "but you are married". The answer is always "I don't care" which is very surprising to me.

The romantic love we are talking about here is not to be confused with romance. Anyone can try to romance anyone else by buying the other person flower, or by telling the other person that you love him/her by telling her/him lies. Romantic love is more part of the essence of lovers.

Eva Peron was another HBBs who demonstrated the link between romantic love and creativity. According to her history, she went from one boyfriend to another until she met her husband who became president of his Argentina for a long period of time after the two met.

Romantic love helps you to have relationships that are far away from violence. In the literature on this kind of love there are all sorts of non-favourable attributes attached to it. For example they say that men and women in romantic love are morbidly dependent, behave as if they were mentally sick that romantic lovers are sadomasochist, that romance itself is a pathological obsession or an addiction, etc. etc. However it is never question of romantic love and violence.

All in all romantic love may be summarized as follows: Positive change agent, creativity enhancer, and organizer of wishes, a health enducer.

In his book *Love That Works*, Bruce Brander sees the love phenomenon under particular lights. According to him there are three levels of love: Eros love, Phyla love and Agape love.

Eros love

What he considers as being Eros love is what I take as romantic love, what would be considered in general as being romantic love? But according to him like a baby love when one HBB in love is very demanding and is expecting to be loved in return. Eros love according to his book leads the intelligent person to seek knowledge, the wise to strive for potential union with the truth, the adventurers to become poets, the inquirers to become investors and scientists. Eros love generates tension to bind, to unite, to blend, and to build. It helps cultivating goodness and nobility. In the book is said also that the exalted level of Eros love is seen as the spirit that created life on earth(How about the Creator?)

Philia Love

According to his book philia love is the love HBBs have when they are married, when everything is divided in half. I'll do, take half of that, you shall do, take the other half. Philia love in his book is like "do Your Part of the Deal" the second of the Four Factors of Happy Long Lasting Relationships that you will see in chapter 8 of this book. In his book it says that "philia love is safe, serene, and long lasting. Yet, it always carries with it the incomplete feeling of a contract. It is a pleasant union, but not union in its fullness"

Agape Love

It is the last level of love between HBBs in relationships. They love and give without expecting something in return. Agape love is freely chosen, free to give or not as it chooses. Eros- lover will die with the beloved; agape-lover will die for the beloved. It is the best and highest form of love that can create "sublime sentiments and actions that we might imagine heaven to offer those who dwell there.

What really kept my being attention awake while reading philia love is that romantic love often leave us with the impression that, despite its imperfect aspects, it is all love can be, that we can go no where else from it, that there can be no other love, and that no other love can be developed from it. I'll bet that many relationships are broken or turn in to violence, because of the false sentiment of completion or a desire for it impossible to satisfy that romantic love creates in HBBs. However, agape- love is exactly that, a form of love developed from eros and philia love.

Bruce Brander says that more often the 3 levels of love shift and blended within us. I would add to that according to the "tank of love" mentioned in the first chapter of this book there are many more kinds of love that are soliciting our attention all the time. The principle is when you are having trouble with one kind of love, it's because another tank of love is empty and needs to be filled. When you are having trouble with sexual love, it's because the tank of parental love or sibling love or friendship love or colleague love is empty and needs to be filled.

One more thing I want to add in this chapter on romantic love and its positive consequences on couples is that the notion of love itself may be less easy to be understood by someone or a society with a too materialistic conception of life, love being really an emotion, untouchable, non physical.

VII

TOWARD SMOOTH
and
SUCCESSFUL RELATIONSHIPS

Rational Valuation

It is that in North American society the emphasis is more on individualism than on partnership. The new phenomenon may be the result of a century of development in psychological studies and an orientation particular to North America. Nonetheless, it has a negative effect on relationships. We are more inclined to avoid it, unconsciously, of course. In other words, it is partly why 50% of marriages end up in divorce nowadays. And we suspect that it is also part of the reason why there are quarrels and even violence between couples in relationships.

Valuation of Partnerships

Therefore for relationships to process smoothly, it is not sufficient to love your partner, but it requires as well that you love relationships as such, it requires that you love to be in relationships. When I was going out with

Debbie, I remember asking myself once if I would become effeminate, if I was with a woman all the time, if I live with or married to a woman. So I may will to be in relationships and at the same time have reason not to be in it for long and that will create negative emotion.

It is already said that there is too much individualism in the new American society (personality cult overflows). This new tendency will definitely kind of backbench relationdhops or put relationships in the last shelve of the library of preoccupation.

A new effort has to be made toward the likeness of partnerships.

It is a bizarre phenomenon, for at first glance, I would say the american societies are to externally oriented, hence too materialist to 'clanistic'. In this context group and partnerships would be their favourite preoccupation. It is a new phenomenon, still un-comprehensible.

The Right Partner

Most of the time HBBs in relationships there are fights because the two members of the couple are not supposed to be together. It happens for many reasons. One of them is that we do not know ourselves that much when we start relationships. When Jeanine and my being were going out together, I know very little of myself in regard to my taste about loving partner. For example, I did not know that I like women with big breasts. It would not be the deciding factor for me even now to marry a woman but it would count, it would be a plus. Ah! Ah! Jeanine was flat "chested" although at that young adult period of my life, I loved Jeanine very much. So the flat "chested" factor must have been in the causality of my fights with her but at the unconscious level at that time.

I discovered only recently that in my essence, meaning in my genes, as a person there is the desire of pacification. Then, this desire would push me toward women of other races to comply with the desire of pacification. Jeanine was the same race than me. I had fight with women of other race also, but of very little significance compare to the ones with Jeanine. They were not venomous; there was no physical violence involved.

I would not advise an HBB to wait until he or she is about to die to get married or enter into an amorous relation, but the adage 'Know thy self", to that could be added easily "Love thy self", applies definitely before entering a rapport in order to avoid too big bumps, in order to avoid violence.

Another reason was suggested to me by Ethel S. Person in *Dreams of Love—Faithful Encounters—The Power of Passion* a book she wrote that I've read. It is that entering such relationships is a very serious enterprise that can last a lifetime. So the choice of the partner requires careful considerations. In other words, if I choose my partner "à la légère", I may die poor for having spent most of my time quarrelling with my partner instead of being inspired by her and the relation, being in jail, or even being dead before my time.

The tendency is to rush into relationships so that we can have sex and/or avoid being alone, avoid ourselves, without paying any attention to the consequence of the action. In other words, if you realize that you have made a mistake, that this person who may be a fine HBB in life, but doesn't correspond to or doesn't have what you really like in the opposite sex, don't try to pick a fight which may deteriorate and become violence. Instead of that just leave. You may leave amiably if you can. If you can not, just pack your bag one day, leave and never to come back, never to get in touch with him/her again, in order to accelerate the process of separation and not suffer too much too long from it.

In *Kickitwell or Else*, the small book I wrote some years ago, there is a chapter or a part on habit formation and deformation, it may help you slip out of relationships, in which you are not happy, before it's too late.

Some love observers are saying now that it is not a right partner to look for but a true partner, someone who is himself or herself. This idea is about the same than mine, but if you like woman with big breast look for her.

Knowing the Fundamental Characteristics of HBBs

In the previous part the emphasis was on knowing yourself first before entering relationships. In this part it will be on knowing HBBs in general including your partner.

Body and Brain and Soul

BODY

Most of the times you hear the words physical body, suggesting that there is a non physical body as well, the mind of the body, sort of, in comparison to the mind in general or the mind in the psyche. Here we are going to consider the physical body, the most precious vehicle a person can have, very important part of relationships. According to what they say, associations between HBBs of the same height and weight are the most common, and, it seems, the happiest and longest.

Nowadays, the attractive woman supposes to be thin. Can it be the cause of violence in in some couples in relationships? Could that be the reason why the process of some liaisons is not smooth at all? It seems that bullies at school pick on the smaller and the thinner of the classes' mates. I can talk about that for having been thin and bullied at school. Apparently, the criminals, also, do not choose the well-built HBBs as the target of their criminal activities. They choose the smallest, the ones who appear weak, fragile and vulnerable, the less younger HBBs. Cougars and lions do that too apparently, they attack the children, the weakest of the herd.

What is sure is that the athletic and healthy women are more attractive than the ones who are not. At least, I myself was more attracted by healthy and athletic woman. Meeting women very often when I was renting 7 bedrooms in a house. After 3 years of love abstinence, I met this woman who rented a bedroom from me. After a short period of time she became my girlfriend. She was very short compare to my own height. I became very much in love with her. I've learned afterward that she was doing physical exercises every morning in her bedroom. Then, I have learned also that she was physically trained in the army. So, it must have been the physical workout in her that attracted me at first.

On *Entertainment Tonight* it was shown a big woman of about 300 pounds and a man who is her boyfriend and who seemed to adore her.

All the above from "body" are to say, underline the importance of good health in relationships and that the absence of it may cause stress, arguments, too big bumps in the in the process of the liaison.

Then, some women are attracted to men with muscle, to athletic men. One girl I tutored once said to me that her boyfriend was an athlete, but he was most of the time to tense, not able to sleep. I concluded that the sexual aspect of her relationships was not great, or, at least, she was not satisfied with it.

Elizabeth Vargas reported a TV show called *20/20* last Friday April 1, 2005 that some boys in teenagers' couples have a violent attitude. I was surprised a bit when I've heard the news, for, first of all, the young couple was not supposed to be in these kinds of deep love and sexual relationships at all. Secondly, there is physical violence in them.

After all, there is a clear explanation for the violence in teenagers who are couple. At that age the animal part of them still has the upper hand in driving them. Then, add deep love and sexual relationships to that is like throwing gasoline on fire. There is already turmoil in them just because it is the way things are at this period of their lives. After that, you adjoin interpersonal relationships; they are in for a rough time. It's like asking them too much too soon.

Among the two teenage couples who were presented in the show, one girl was physically assaulted; the other is dead. The two boys were athletic men.

In regard to athletic HBBs, there is no sufficient evidence to conclude on the quality of their relationships, but athletism for athletism in couples is ground for very big bumps or violence in the course of these rapports. When choosing a partner, you will think of that. Right!

It's up to authorities to decide what precise age it should happen, but if men of 20 years old and more don't know women anatomy and the mechanism of sexuality (a complete picture where penetration can happens, doesn't happen), we didn't do a good job in educating them, we have a problem.

However, being educated in human anatomy at the proper age, when sexuality may happen will create smoothness in relationships.

BRAIN

This physical part of the body is not sensible to us in the sense that if a HBB could touch our brain we wouldn't be able to feel it. They make brain surgery on patient in hospital. They are able to talk at the same time as if nothing is happening to them.

I am going to refer to the mind of the body in the body part of this chapter, the brain being part of the body, therefore, is part of the mind of the body (neurons, cells, similar to elemental level).

Being the center of all our motor functions, this organ fascinate us, but it is not the center of intelligence for example, otherwise, elephant would be more intelligent than human beings for having a much bigger brain than us. The fascination with the brain affects negatively even in Psychiatry where name of mental sicknesses derived from the brain. I am thinking of schizophrenia. The part phrenia in the word stand for brain in Greek.

So the brain is not the mind should not be confused with it, If you do you will die of all sort bizarre illnesses called functional diseases for which supposedly there are no cure. Brain is physical; mind is not. Brain is part of the body; mind is part of the psyche. Brain is the center of the motor functions; mind is relevant to mental functions. The relation between the two is similar to the relation between water and electricity, the first causes the latter, but the two are not of the same nature.

When we can differentiate between fundamental parts of ourselves, when we are clear within ourselves, our external relations are clear, all that will certainly promote relationships between couples.

SOUL

There are many definitions related to soul. I remember a few of them: Soul or esthetic body meaning soul is body becoming substance. I call it asterisk because the images I am having about it are bizarre, without a fixed form. I call it Genio, the name of my nephew or my genius part. However, it is also in our environment, in trees why HBBs hug tree in Cluquote Sounds Sound and animals. Soul is also our guide, the one who pushes us to do more.

The Soul of the World is at as international level.

For more information please see *The Soul Exposed*, another book that I wrote.

Psyche and Mind

Psyche

GENERAL DEFINITION

The definition of Jean Paul Sartre of the psyche: In-Itself, For-Others, and For-Self- En-Soi, Pour-Autrui, Pour-Soi- is incomplete for one doesn't see where fit the components of the psyche such as the will, the mind, the intuition in such definition, And then, it does not seem similar to the definition of other observers who see the psyche as layers of organic energy. However it gives us a solid ground on which to place our view on it as related to couples in relationships. So, below, we are going to review each part of the definition to find out how they may connect to couple in liaison, if they promote it or not.

IN-SELF

This part of human psyche unites us with the physical world and allows us to create natural sciences and expanding our knowledge of them. It goes from the Stone Age to the age of advance technology, from stone as instrument to computer, space shuttle (and trip to the moon). We may observe nowadays a distance from nature at the root of which is the attraction of life in big cities where there are noise, pollution, where we have too many activities to do, where we have television with too many canals to watch, Life in big cities is taking away from us our humanity. Nonetheless, In-Self, this part of the psyche has served us well (or we have used it well enough) even though the knowledge of nature will never be complete. And what is good for all HBBs on the planet is good also for couples in relationships.

FOR-OTHERS

In one hand, the same can be said for this other part of the psyche, also, which refers to other HBBs and society as a whole. We go from life in holes in mountain to rural life and to life in big cities like Paris, New York, Berlin etc. In the big cities there are all sort of services offered by many communities sponsored by governments, the private sector and voluntary workers.

In regard to work we go from little confreres (brotherhood) organizations to big syndicalism, big corporate.

In this regard life of couples in relationships has flourished. There are all sorts of social progressions and arrangements to make things better for couples, to make it possible for them to live an authentic life.

In the other hand, as far as "for others" is concerned there are some misdirections during its historical transformation or the historical development of humanity in regard to "For Others"? In other words, things haven't been unfolded so positively, for almost our entire attention is directed toward others while we forget ourselves. The result is that our selves stay undeveloped, "For others" development becomes "against others development". That part of the psyche expansion (or our expansion in regard to it) becomes having power over others and trying to dominate them, trying to be in control. In that sense "For Others" growth doesn't serve society at large neither individual, neither couples in relationships, instead, it is the cause for concern, the cause for violence between members of couples.

Imagine having the whole society trying to manipulate you unconconciously.

FOR-SELF

This part of our psyche is relevant to us to our individuality. As we just said, we do not grow in regard to it as much as it could be, because our attention is grabbed almost totally by the other two parts of the psyche. The "For-Self" stays in its natural state meaning unspecified, disorganized.

Of course there is some progress after a hundred years or so of study on the self, a hundred years or so since the foundation of psychology. After all, the psychological world, the psychological economy, the world of private properties, to be precise, the capitalist economy as so far won over the communist economy, signed by the collapse of the soviet bloc.

However, in the horizon we can see coming the negative effects of too much individualism. The emphasis on individualism is such that young women and young men in the new American society behave as if their parents did not bring them up. It because they have been left alone so that they can develop their independency missing then the stage in their growth process when the love of the parents, taking care by the parents are still necessary. They have been pushed to independency too soon.

I was in grade 8 in secondary school, my father said to me that it was time for me to go on my own, withdraw all financial support that he used to give me. Up to then I was among the firsts in the classes. Since then, my grade became not so famous until I move out of the country.

The problem of young boys left alone to themselves was underlined by Laura Bush in an interview with Barbara Walters a day before the American presidential inauguration.

Too much emphasis on individualism or the "overindidualism" creates an unproductive competitive tendency, competition where we suppose to have collaboration. That is why I sent a letter to the Canadian Parliament, addressed to Prime Minister Martin, to Mr. Steven Harper, and to Mr. Jack Layton, at the head of the conservative and the democratic party, asking them to put some water in their wine and not jump to the first occasion to call another Canadian election. In other words I was asking them to cooperate.

The "overindividualism" mentioned above is in fact a push toward the external power. When my father said to me that I was on my own, he didn't mean that he let me on my own to study myself. He meant that I should go in the world outside to earn my life, that I should quit school and go to work. It was not a push toward self-specification, which is really the aim of psychology.

The Mind

Although the mind has been used for the psyche. One of the negative consequences of that is functional diseases such as multiple sclerosis, Alzheimer, Parkinson. Another one is a world shrink for using the part instead of the whole, for mind is only a component of psyche. The psyche itself may never be completely understood. We know, however, about it what we have said above and that the mind, the will, the intuition, the imagination, memory, are part of the psyche and everyone and everything-this last word is a stretched, but I am allowed to make it.

Yesterday in a page in the Internet they ask me to answer a question on category that was said this way "which one doesn't belong to the group?" It was a few vowels and one consonant. After that they asked to take a test on IQ. I skipped that one and left the page. The IQ measurement proves that even psychologists are confused about the mind.

I look in the *French and English Dictionary* by J. E. Mansion, M.A. that I have. There is a column of about 8 inches on the word mind where mind means memory, thinking, idea, intention, etc. from expressions in the day to day language. Only in one expression mind means head and that is "He is off his mind". Because in French it means Il a perdu la tête (He had lost his head). But according to that dictionary, mind is never confused with the psyche, meaning that in the ordinary day to day language mind is not confused with the psyche.

Then, I look in the thesaurus in the computer where it said that mind means brain. Beside that it gives a list of synonyms for mind: brain, intelligence, intellect, wits, brains, brainpower, psyche, mentality.

From that list, we can strike off brain, wits, and psyche, because they don't belong to the same category. As said above the correlation between the brain and the psyche is the same as the correlation between water and electricity. Can we say then water and electricity are synonymous? Of course not.

The strangeness of it all is that in ordinary daily life mind doesn't seem to be confused with or taken for brain, wits or psyche while it is in the intellectual world.

The way I see it is that mind is psychological processor, like one small natural, human computer. The biggest natural and human computer should be in the intuition if it's not intuition itself. Intuition is in the psyche, not in the mind.

The reason why it is important to sort out those parts of human beings is multiple fold. The most obvious and urgent reasons are treatment. For if someone's sickness is related to his body and that we look for it in his mind or in his brain, we will not be able to treat that person, and vice versa, if the illness is in the psyche, we look only in the body we will not be able to find the treatment for that person either. That's why some cancers and the functional diseases are said to be incurable.

The second most obvious and urgent reason to sort out those parts of human beings is related to freedom, to the betterment of our lives, related to the use of all parts of ourselves, to extend our possibilities, to become more human.

In such atmosphere individuals are rather cool calm and collected. Couples in relationships have more options. They don't rely on doubtful technique as the symbolization of ambivalence to put some zest in their relation. They have a clear mind; most of the time they are in good mood. They do not play a role. They stay themselves most of the time. Love is of value to them. Their love for each other is continuously renewed. The life of their liaison is endless.

The Impossibility to Possess Others

That brings us the question: Who is a human being? If another planet on which there are living beings similar to us existed, you go there, they ask you to describe a human being, what would you say? Are we a body, a psyche, an information, what we know, what we possess? The answer to the question can take many forms dependent on who you ask. If you ask someone with a background on physical studies, he will say that we are energy. The religious person would say we are a mind or spirit. The physician would say we are a body. Some psychologists say we are energy and information.

The definition of human beings that is adopted in other psychology is, "we are a center of self-consciousness, a center of will capable of guiding, mastering and utilizing all-almost- of our psychological processes and our body". Self-consciousness and will are the key of the definition, but they are not substantial, They are not like something you can touch and measure. In other words, we have a body that is very important to us that carries us around, that can be touched, that can be kept in jail, but the real person in us cannot be touched with hands, cannot be kept in jail, cannot be possessed. You cannot possess what is not purely substantial.

According to my being we are body, soul and spirit. Yes we are concious of ourselves, but consciousness cannot define us for the bigger parts of ourselves are not conscious. The Creator is also part of us but, a definition of human beings in which the Creator is not included misses the boat, is incomplete.

When abused women say that "you can have my body but you do not have me" that is what they mean. Love can be obtained by love but not by force. It is also an expression of the non substantial part of HBB.

Sometimes, I think that the problem not easy to solve. While in relationships one must not to identify with the other person, one must stay oneself and blend with the other person at the same time.

Self Identification

1. Self Identification in General

In long distance relationships with Mihaela of Bulgaria for about a year in 2002, I sent her what I thought was a nice e-mail explaining what self-identification is about. In her answer to me she said that she didn't understand a word of it. I hope this time it will be better, that after reading it in the book you will feel a bit happier, or, at least, you will not feel disappointed as Mihaela was. For, you already have an idea what the psyche and the self are in the part you have just read above in the "center of self-consciousness- one person defines the self as all that we possess including feelings- a center of will capable of guiding, mastering and utilizing all our psychological processes all our body".

In life in general we may identify with anyone and or anything we like, love, value, anything we do, use most of the time. For example, we may identify with our parents. The physician may identify with medicine; the teacher may identify with teaching. Up to here, it is less likely to be unclear, because one can say we not only identify with our parents, we are them. That what it looks like when we say everybody is responsible for what happened to him or her-not always- What happened to you is part of your psychological make up. In the case of child, or even an adolescent still leaving with their parents, they are not even able to feed themselves. How will they be responsible in a car accident? Of course they are not, but their parents are. That is why we may say we are our parents. So identification with parents is clear although wrong.

Most mothers see themselves as a mother first and for most. In reality, she just a woman who has kids. She can live the life of full woman, having a profession, working or staying at home taking care of her children and of herself, in other words, enjoying herself, her life. No, because she is a mother, she doesn't have the right to be enjoying herself, even if her children and her husband are equally happy according to social dictate. It's like having children is signing a contract to be miserable since she identified with motherhood instead of identifying with herself.

Less clear is when we identify with our profession, which are not a person but a thing. Jake is the president of a country. His country invades another one. Jake identifies so much with politics that his character is reflected in the battlefield during the invasion. For respect of privacy, I cannot have all the details, but it does happened in complete life, it is a waking life situation. One other HBB identifies with her name so much that it killed her.

The main problem with identification with anything or anybody else than self is that what you identify with controls you .If you identify with your religious God, it controls you. If you identify with your parents, they control you. If you identify with your lover or beloved she or he controls you. Then, it means you are not in charge of your lives. You are no more a responsible person. You become irresponsible, living like a child or a pet or puppet. Anything can happen to you when you are not identified with yourself.

The worse identification is with physical things such as cars, boats, houses (identification is not equal to liking, but it's easy to identify to what you like). The best that could be said with this kind of identification is that human body being physical, identification with physical things is identification with the human body. Up to now everything seems to be ok, but the big difference is that our body is also spiritual at the cellular level. In this book and above we mentioned "the spirit of the body". Otherwise, given that physical things are not living beings, are in a state that will decay, identify with them is like identifying with sicknesses and death.

Self Identification in Regard to Couples

I always have the impression that most relationships fail because of the effort it takes to sort out who we are and stay whom we are while in relationships.

It is very easy to identify with the person with whom we are in a relationships, the person we love. Not wanting to be alone all by yourself, you get into relationships, you find someone to be with, to share your life with. It is very likely that you will identify with that person who fills the gap in you. So, some relationships are doom from the start. They are spoiled in two ways, by the void in one member of the couple, and by identification with the other member of the couple.

In other words to be able to love the other person, we must first love ourselves. To be able to be in relationships that are not too bumpy, relationships without violence with that person, we must first be able to be with ourselves and learn to identify with ourselves.

   1.   How to be with someone else and identify with self

We are referring to the moments spent not thinking about work, partners, other HBBs you are comparing yourself with and whom you would like to emulate. We are referring to moments when you are alone and wouldn't like to be with someone else either. We are referring to these moments when you are thinking of one thing or to nothing in particular. We are referring to these moments of meditation. In other words, the idea you have on how to meditate in this book or in any other book, will help, also, toward acquiring the ability to spend moments without the rush to open the radio, the TV, other devices in the house to keep busy, without the need to be in the outside world for a moment

In regard to the self identification part, you can make a list of the things or HBBs you are most likely to identify with such as your parents, your boss, your partners, your work, your car, your boat, and so on. Then you can take 20 minutes a day, twice a week, a week, depending on the amount of free time you have, thinking of not to identify with these HBBs or things, but to identify with yourself, the person you really are (the ability to be oneself should have been developed at one year old, but it is not done yet in our societies).

There are work, careers, goals, all sort obligations that will keep you attention busy, and all sorts of temptations by less important things to identified with. The exercise in self-identification is a life time process.

Self-identification is not individualization, or "overindividualization" (allusion is made to that above) as it is observed in North America. The fundamental cause of "overindividualization" (or lack of cooperation or selfishness or too competitive) is the competition in a market economy. "Overindividualization" is an external and new phenomenon, may be only in part of the world, not everywhere. Identification with things and other HBBs (not identified with self) has been on since a long time ego everywhere in the world.

When you are really yourself, the Creator is included as well as everything and everyone else.

Pleasure and Successful Relationships

It reminds me of the little book of Sark "Eat Mango Naked" in which she states that you can have pleasure any time. HBBs in Titanic continued having fun even after learning that the boat hit an iceberg. Sark's statement makes so much sense that it becomes banal. If it so, then why is it so difficult to have fun without feeling guilty or unease somehow? Evil instinct? We divide pleasure in two parts: pleasure obtained from the absence of pain and the input of pleasure. Let's see how they can enlighten us on the answer of the question.

1. Pleasure Obtained After Pain

Watching one of the Tara Bank shows on the search for the cover girl, I did not realize why a man who were taking photos of the girls while they are playing tennis were so rude with them by telling them very unpleasant words such as "You do not make sense. That posture is not nice at all". At the end of the sequence of activity, he told them he was playing a role that he was asked to behave that way. At that time I realize what was going on. It was a session of aggressiveness for love (should we say for motivation, given that emotion is motivation), because after they aggressively demean them, the girls theatrically suppose to feel happy. Pleasure should follow the aggressive exercise.

At the American Idol shows the same observation can be made. Simon one of the judges has a reputation of being rude with the contestant. Why? To create passion in them for the career they have chosen by the pleasure the sadness will create in them afterward. In that sense, the contestants should praise him for being rude with them.

The psychological phenomenon is known by HBBs from a long time, has been observed in intellectual psychological circle. In the time of the glory of Roma, couples used to watch the gladiators to instill love in each other for each other. In Robert C. Beck Book on motivation, he cites Klein who "concentrates upon element of hate within loving relationships, but also treats it as motive that propels one individual from one level of love to another".

"The most elevated love", apparently, "occurs as an escape from the hurtfulness of aggressive attitude in self and as compensation for them".

Using aggression for love, however, leave me perplexed for many reasons. One of them is that it may be why it is difficult to have pleasure without a sense of having done something wrong (in fact we did something in most cases), consciously or unconsciously. Another reason is we may think we can have pleasure continuously given that we can create it at will by the use of aggression and we may raise the level of aggressivity for more pleasure. Once we start raising the level of aggression, who knows where it will stop? Beating and killing? We are in the sheer field of crime, aren't we? For there is such a thing as being addicted to pleasure. This is a way to explain mental sicknesses such as masochism, sadomasochism.

We have in the above paragraph one part of the answer of our question that is to say that the guilty conscience created for having pleasure is caused by link between pleasure and aggression- as Freud would say as two instincts opposing each other.

Then, there is also that intense feelings create its opposite, all things that advise caution with pleasure obtain from aggressive behaviour, caution about producing pleasure just for the sake of it.

Other part of the answer is in that sexual pleasure is a very powerful one, but that not everybody can have sex, and society places some taboos on it.

2. Pleasurable Input

It is the simple kind of pleasure, it is also created at will, can be used by any member of couples any time. There not supposed to be negative side effect. It is the pleasure we create in the other person when we buy him/her gifts, flower, teddy bear, pleasure that we form in her/him when we are kind toward her, bring her to movies, theatre, when we go to dance with her/him, when we take her/him for a ride in car or in a boat, and so on.

It's a pleasure I generate by practicing generating it. As said above, there is social taboos against pleasure that make us feel guilty by having pleasure. So becoming an expert in generating it will not come just by the desire. In other words you just have to do it again, and again, and again, until it becomes automatic, your most faithful companion. Then you know how to level the ups and downs of "la vie à deux", how to keep being in relationships when it is desired.

Knowing ourselves better helps us to know others better. In this context, the possibilities for having quarrels in our relationships are reduced to the minimum, the possibilities for violence even less than that. Then, in this chapter of "Relation Amoureuse" in particular, there are different differentiations: the brain, the mind, the psyche, motor functions, mental functions, all goodies that will permit us to live longer in love.

Management of Feelings

Introduction

The members of the couple love each other, nevertheless they are quarrelling very often, and they are fighting very often. How can you create such negative feelings in someone you love and how can someone you love generates such negative feelings in you?

We have seen that, in the first chapter, Arnold and Anne Marie quarrel with each other very often, that I loved Jeanine still hit her once badly.

Last Thursday May 5, 2005, When I arrived at Harwin's, a grade 10 student whom I tutor, I find him in terrible bad moment yelling at his sister very loudly. Later, he explained to me that his sister accused him of taking her things and that he told her he did not do it but she continued accusing him. Later, after asking him a few questions, he was afraid that when she starts accusing him she would not stop. In other words he was yelling, because he may be afraid he would not be able to make her stop. He was afraid of both of them becoming out of control.

Harwin is only 15 years old, Jagwin, his sister, is about 9 or 10 years old. It's normal for them to be like that, for Harwin not to be able to control his emotions, to manage his feelings. Psychology is only taught in colleges, even then it's not about managing emotions. It's less easy to figure out why adults in love fight, especially the ones in sexual and love relationships (hatredness underneath love, bizarre).

Steps

1. So, the first step in managing your emotion is to get familiar with it by reading about it.

Plus what you have read in literature on emotion you want to retain, remember also this: that actions and thoughts are behind emotion, in other words, there are a circular and causal relation between emotion, thought and action. Then what you say to yourself will be behind your emotions and your actions, remember that too.

You may not find this in libraries, for the little book, which inspired it, is not very young. It's called *The Lazy Man Way to Riches* and written by Joe Karbo. In a few steps to create the right attitude to get rich he says more or less (It has been rearranged by me): Contact, feel, and easily show your emotion to yourself and all other HBBs (human beings becoming). If you are angry, show it and thus release it. If you are happy show this. If you are sad you'll find it easy to weep and thus release the sadness. The ability to show emotion at appropriate time and place is extremely valuable and the mark of a mature person.

2. Take a deep breathe and

3. Take it easy; emotion, as the word (motion) indicates is a passing sensation (lingers only when there is problem around it, at that time it is called feeling). Most of the time by waiting a few seconds, something else might come up that attract your attention. By that time the emotion is already gone even if it was negative.

4. I have goals; to reinforce them I do what is called daily declaration, which consists of a text in which, the goals are described briefly, and that I say to my self before falling asleep at night, and first thing in the morning. In my daily declaration there is a sentence serving at controlling a little bit negative emotion. It goes like that: "I have proportional emotion related to the theories and practices that I do not use in order not to reinforce them inadvertently". It can help anybody in the management of emotions domain.

5. The sibling technique

    * Buy a card.

    * Write down what the other person does to you that you like.

    * Write down what the other person does to you that you don't like or makes you mad.

    * Next time same kind of conflict arises, ask the person to read the card again.

6. Action Instead of Reaction

Observe in what circumstances you have strong emotional reaction with him/her; observe what exactly she/he says, doesn't say, doesn't do that generates strong emotion in you; observe also when these strong emotions happen. Then find out what you're going to do the next time you will be in the same situation to prevent yourself from having uncontrollable reaction. In that case, you will act instead of react.

7. Open the Door

The previous steps will help you to have a little bit of control over your emotion in order not to loose it with the person you are in a love relationships with, will help you not to become an emotional wreckage each time you face a new challenge. However, that is not enough, with the background above, you will be able to open the door to all your love potentials (by telling that to yourself often for a certain period of time) in other for them to show up in your lives in their positive forms. In other words restricted love potential create troubles in relationships, liberated love potentials brings dynamism and peace in relationships. After that the situation which used to trigger mad mood, becomes a mild irritation, even an occasion for love. The situation which used to bring you up and down, becomes a stimulation

Most of the time we short the door to our potentials, because we fear that it would be dangerous to let them loose. The when you short the door at them, that is exactly the way they will come out, with their negative form, that is where the danger is really in relationships, by closing the door to your loving potentials.

VIII

SUCCESSFUL RELATIONSHIPS

What Are Successful Relationships?

It seems that this question would have as many different answers as there are individuals. For some of you successful relationships would be the ones in which both members of the couple become wealthy, in which both members od the couple are healthy. For some others, it could be relationships in which both members of the couple are happy. Still for some others it could be relationships that last. But for the purpose of this book we are going to retain happy and lasting. In other words for the purpose of this book successful relationships are the one in which there are happiness and continuation.

We do not say that that there is no violence in the happy relationships, because happiness implies that.

The Love Factors:
the Reasons why 50% of Marriage Are
Successful According to Researches:

1. Sharing friendships and love

2. Treating each other with kindness and respect

3. Doing your part of the deal

4. Commitment

Sharing Friendship and Love

Adolescent and young adult, I used to spend hours and hours talking with friends. It true that at that time I thought, as most adolents do, I could solve all of the problems of the world, there is no reason why a version of this adolescent attitude cannot be applied to relationships. I spend time with my friends, I know them better, they know me better and most importantly I know myself better. Knowing yourself better helps you make better choices in your life.

A friend is somebody who accepts me all the way and sombody I accept all the way. So I can be myself with him/her and they can be themselves with me. That creates an atmosphere for growth between the two personalities (we still have to avoid familiarity. It is poison to sexual attraction).

One of my friends got himself in trouble with police sometimes. He even used me to get himself out of these kinds of trouble once. To this day I would never think of doing something that could hurt him. A friend is a friend is a friend.

All that describes an atmosphere very far away from violence and destruction, very close to peace, love and life.

Treating Each Other with Kindness and Respect

This one of the four factors of successful relationships observed by researchers appears to be a simple thing, but it is not. Kindness alone has been interpreted in many ways such as compassion, sympathy gentleness, kind heartedness, benevolence, thoughtfulness, humanity, consideration, and helpfulness.

Being compassionate toward your love one(s) is like a pleonasm, for love seems to mean exactly that. The way I understand compassion is to feel what the other person is feeling. I am happy or sad when the other person is happy or sad. In other words the events that affect the person affect me too.

Sympathy is sharing ideas with your love one; some of my ideas about life are the same. In my individual belief system there are some points common to sympathy.

Gentleness: Last Christmas time, I was about to go in a line up in a pharmacy at about the same time than a nice looking young lady. I was a bit in front of her, but I let her get in front of me. She paid for the few things she had bought and bought me a scratch ticket. I kept the ticket for about 3 months to remind myself of her and her gentleness toward my being.

Then, about two months ago, I went to a big supermarket, bought two items, a packages of hotdog, and another item I thought I knew, but did not know what it was really, either its price. I had a few hundred dollars in the house, brought with me in the supermarket very little money than what I was supposed to pay for the two items. Because there was an unknown item in what took from the shelves, not only I had to spend all the money I got, but also I was about $2 short. I was so embarrassed. I wanted to leave one item. But, there was a lady behind me who said that she pay for them and she did.

All this time I did not know what was happening, if I had bought an unknown item, what I have realized only later when I came back home. The day later I brought the unknown item back to the store, they gave me the money spent for it.

If we behave that way in relationships, we're in for paradise on earth. That does not exist really, but it's ok.

Benevolence: the most common understanding we have of benevolence is related to voluntary work. I have done my share of voluntary work. The important ones were for ministry of health in British Columbia and for BC Teachers Federation. At the ministry of health, we all were trying to reform the health system to make it better for everyone. I quit when I realize that there was too much politics, too much egos there and that there would not be much of an amelioration until we teach each individual to take their own health matter in their own hands, that there could be a place for privatization of health in Canada an then government would not have to pay for it, would only have to regulate the private sector. That said without including the Creator in our lives, observing It to ground it truth which is , in fact, our truth, nothing goes.

At the federation I was working with unemployed Teachers, again a federation of egos. "On est pas sorti du bois", or we are not out of the wood yet.

Humanity: I always have the impression that when we succeed in relationships, in association and in love, it is because as a human being we have grown up. We have developed human being qualities that allow us to associate with each other. We have a positive attitude toward human being in general, not just the particular individual who we love. In my particular vocabulary there is no such thing as people but HBB, which stand for human being human becoming.

Thoughtfulness: That is to always have the other person in mind in our daily life in order for our decisions and actions not to hurt the person with whom we are in a relationships, our girlfriends, and our boyfriends. Our husbands, wives and associates. It can go up to anticipating the other person's need in other to satisfy him and make him happy. The basic principle in thoughtfulness is to figure out how the love one would react toward all you actions and decisions.

Consideration: Being considerate is being delicate, lovely and regardful in order not to put the person you love in embarrassing situations. In May 2005, I've been to New York and spent few days with a brothers I did not see for a long time. One of the days while I was there was the birthday of his wife. She said to me that her husband never gave her anything on her birthday. The day before her birthday I bought some flower and a card. To be non-considerate I would just give them to my brother's wife. It would put my brother in an embarrassing situation. I gave the card and the flower to him and asked him to give them to his wife on her birthday.

Helpfulness: Most HBBs will not have a problem with this successful factor of relationship. Not only it's an easy concept to understand, also to apply. I remember when I was about to break up with Debbie she was still trying to help me financially. If she was trying to help at that time when things were bad between us, You can imagine how much she was ready to help when we were having good time together.

Helpfulness is a little bit similar to benevolence.

It is a concept, which is well entrenched in most societies. Everywhere you go you see HBBs collecting money for such or such organization which is itself trying to help one group of HBBs or another. Often you see on TV, or hear on the radio shows set up just to collect money to help finding a solution of a human problem. So it would be rare for relationships to fail because the members of the couple did not try to help each other, because they do not have a helpful attitude(the attitude becomes exaggerated in America, sometimes, the collector seems more interested in the idea of collecting than the HBBs they are collecting it for, of course they are collecting for a cause, but that cause always linked to HBBs, sometimes I think they are jus collecting votes to accumulate political capital)

We are still at the same successful factor of relationships that is treating each other with kindness and respect, but this time we are about to elaborate on respect. For you bet it the heaviest cause of failure in relationships. Some observers of love think that most men cannot really love women. Because they are so much in power and competition trip, they are unable to respect women who they see as being inferior to themselves, as we're already said in this book. The same observation can be made also for relationships.

It is not clear why, but in general, it is not an easy task to respect another person, especially when the other is close to us. We get used to him/her; we take her/him for granted. Most of the time, we are unconsciously saying to ourselves that we have no value, therefore if the person live with us or is married with us it is because her or he too has no value, and consequently doesn't deserve our respect.

The Japanese and the Vietnamese seem to have a developed sense of respect for other human being entrenched in their societies, in their culture. I am not sure if I am creating a stereotype by writing that for not having been neither in Japan nor Vietnam yet, the bowing custom is definitely a sign of great respect for other HBBs.

Most HBBs of developed countries would not score well in this regard. They would score well rather in a contest of spoiled brat and that is not sign of a sense of respect for other HBBs. Anyway, respect for each other is one way a relationship will fail or endure, according to researches.

Doing Your Part of the Deal

It is not clear to me how the researchers process this factor of successful relationships in their books or thought system, but it is related to physical aspects of liaison. Most of the time it will be men go to work outside, women take care of the household, although nowadays there could be some variation. If there is not any accident or big social or economical turmoil, this factor of successful relationships shouldn't not constitute a problem difficult to solve. Although it will depend on which level of love we are in the relationships. If we are at the first level of love, called romantic love, called also "baby love", we might say "gi'me, gi'me, gi'me" because we want to take, take, take. So they're maybe some tendency to imbalance in regard to task responsibility in the relationships. If we are at the level of philia" love, there could not be non-proportional tendencies, because at this stage of love that is what we do. We share things squarely. If we are at the "agape" stage, again there can be imbalance, although a positive one this times, because it's a kind of love when we give from the heart, without expecting something in return.

Doing your part in the relationships according the agreement you have had with your partner is clear-cut concept? There is no possibility for misinterpretation, to make mistake about it.

Commitment

Being successful in "la vie a deux" is similar with creating a goal somehow. Let say you have the goal to buy an expansive car today. Tomorrow, you are asking yourself if you really need an expansive car. You make an effort on yourself and keep the goal, and specify it a bit by adding the type of the expensive car you want to buy. Two weeks later, you change your mind on the type. Two weeks later again, you change your mind about it again. You don't have to be brilliant to know that you would never be able to create the goal that way, that there is a serious inner objection to the creation of that goal.

The same is true for relationships. If both partners do not have fixed idea on it, if both members of the couple can not say to themselves that they are in it and want to stay in it, then there will be big problems, quarrels, and fights. In other words these kind of relationships are dangerous can make the life of the couple miserable and can even cost one of them or both of them their lives.

Obstacles Against Commitment

Commitment, also, is a clear-cut concept, but members of couples will not commit that easily for various reasons. There are the social obstacles and individual obstacles against it. In regard to social obstacles there is the Don Juan value discussed in the first part of the book. There is also negative vibration coming mainly from the agents of the commerce of love and relationships, which is a huge market.

Young HBBs will not commit that easily for various reasons of their own including that they are at the beginning of their lives they want to explore what is out there. And that at that age possibilities of forming a couple are endless, so staying in one relationship is difficult. Then, also, it easy to think that it's going to stay that way all the time, that we will be able to find a partner almost every day, that we are not going to grow old physically speaking, as if the pill for eternal life is already discovered.

That the way I was. I went from relationships to relationships without ever thinking of committing for a second. I was too busy living for that. What was important for me then was the number of relationships not the relationships themselves.

Social, Economic and Political Context

Social Context

It said that Japanese and some other groups of HBBs of the world are not able to experience really romantic love, because of the individual aspect of that kind of love. Meaning in Japan, the emphasis is rather on the group as whole instead of being on the individuals.

However, Western male individuals, also, apparently, are unable to experience romantic love, for they are too competitive. And that goes against one of the fundamental characteritics of romantic love, that is to say, surrendering.

In any which way we turn it, we will find that the social context not only influences the way we love, but also tend to define it squarely. Then we are allowed to conclude that violence in couple underlines violence in society, although the purpose here is not to do sociology, to elaborate on social issues.

Economic Context

One of the reasons why there are fights in relationships is linked to money problem as stated in preamble. From there one may conclude that richness favours relationships and that poverty does not.

What is bizarre is that richness favours sexual relationships between HBBs, and not necessarily procreation or love. India and China are the most populous countries in the world (although they are becoming rich now, my thinking is that they will become less populated as well), but they are not necessarily the richest, In the other hands, the rich countries are not the most populous.

When we are rich or wealthy, we have less moments to be unhappy, and more moments to be happy, that may reduce the possibility for violence in relationships. Still, it is not safe to count on that sort of rationalizarion to explain violence absence of it in relationships, the small idea in psychology is that richness does not create our emotions, or feelings, but only amplify them.

Political Context

Some societies favour association or relationships more than others do as it is already said above.

Would marriage flourishes in a dictator state? It seems that it would if the dictator favors marriage. In a state like that you do what you supposed to do. But in reality it would not, for according to a principle in psychology behaviour change instigated by self is what is maintained not behaviour brought about by external forces or agent. In other words in the dictator state where the dictator favours marriage, it would be accepted for a time and dropped afterward, marriage having been dictated to the citizens.

How about a democratic state? Would relationships succeed in such context? It reminds us of Pierre Trudeau who said the state has nothing to do in the bedroom of its citizens.

Researches show that in our Western democratic states, only 50% of marriages succeed.

In almost all societies in the world presently external power is the value. What is its consequence on relationships? I think that the rate of marriage is so low not only because of liberal attitude in democratic societies, but also by external power which becomes the wrong social value. Everyone is trying to become Prime Minister. Everyone is trying to control the other person. It is bad for good individuality(not the crazy one observed in North America), and bad for sexual relationships.

Individual Makeup

1. Individual characteristic or personality

Two brothers of mine are married and are of the same father and mother. The marriage of the younger one is successful according to the definition of successful relationships as stated above. The less young brother's marriage is not so successful. The younger one is 6 feet plus tall, corpulent. The older one is 5 feet and 8 or 9 inches tall and less of a body total volume than the younger brother is. Can that be why they have different result of relationships? Can the physical difference be accounted for the different result of their relationships?

Then, the tallest, corpulent and imposing brother (in the winning liaison) marries a woman who is very short, may be 4 feet and something. The other brother who is in a "non-victorious" wedding is about the same height than his wife or is just a little taller than his wife. Is the "successful marriage" is caused by the physical size discrepancy between the two members of that couple? For some of relationship observers, there is definitely an element of power in lasting sexual relationships.

There is probably a link between the physical and psychological makeup of individuals. But is the relationship of the person who is more outgoing better or worst than the person who is less outgoing?

2. Individual Mental Development

In the sense that the HBB with a psyche more or less developed would fair better in the relationship field than the one with a psyche less developed. The person with his/her psyche more developed will have a better grip of the emotions that the ups and downs in his/her life are bound to create during the days of their living together.

The person with a lesser mental (What you call spiritual development) will have a tendency to banish emotions in his life. When he does have emotions, he will not be able to control them. So, or he is split inside, functioning with the bare minimum in terms of psychic tools he is born with but unable to use or he is at war against himself. Not only he will fair less in terms of success in relationships, but also violence is more likely to be reflected in it, for his negative inner state would have a tendency to surface in his complete life.

IX

SUCCESSFUL RELATIONSHIPS

Contact

Arthur C. Wosner wrote a book called *Making Contact* in which he describes the negative effect of lack of contact on some of us. According to him the lack of contact is created by shyness and negative self-image. It prevents the shy person from hearing what others are really saying in situation where relationships could be initiated and developed.

The kind of contact he describes includes a lot of positive and loving moves toward the other person such as sending her flower, buying him a gift, touching her as an act of love, etc.

The author writes "The deterioration of contact in marriage is in my estimate the most common marital problem occurring more often then incidence of adultery, physical brutality, financial mismanagement, sexual incompatibility combined".

The Inclusion of Sophia the Soul of the World and the Creator in the Relationships

This point may be illustrated by Angelina Jolly (Madonna to a certain extent, and other like them we do not know). I am not sure if Angelina is really conscious of what she is doing by adopting many babies, but the implication is she is going to have LASTING RELATIONSHIPS. By adopting babies, she is including Sophia and the Creator in her love relationships (according to soul psycholohy).

Because it is not known if she is conscious of what she is doing by adopting babies, it is not known either if her relationships with Brad will last. Possibly it should, however if you are not conscious of a process, you may stop doing exactly what makes it work.

Then, Including Sophia the Soul of the World in the relationships as the third element of the love triangle does not necessarily means adopting babies, could mean something completely different such as helping poor HBBs in the world. The essential matter here seems to be that the loving endeavour must be related to the rest of the world.

For more information on Sophia, please Read Robert Sadello in *Love and the World*.

If relationships are working, are based on the mastering of contact, the inclusion of Sophia, the Creator the seed of violence is vanished and gone.

Why the Need for Happy and Lasting Relationships?

To have peace in the family which can concur to social and world peace. One of my goals is to be able to organize one day what could be called THE HUMANIMNIZING DAYS in order to celebrate HBBs with emphasis on the total human being not just the physical part of us, and the Creator in the background, no worshiping. Living life normally is worshiping enough, if we stay close to the Creator in our thinking.

1. To keep having HBBs on earth, Canada and some other countries legalize marriage between same sex. I will not take

side on this topic. I do not have any solid argument on why they should nor why they should not. One thing is that the recognition of this kind of relationships will make crime against homosexual less appealing. But we have to be careful, for life on earth can be eliminated by procreation zero as well as by atomic bomb. It is OK to leave each individual who is not committing crime to live their life peacefully regardless of their sexual orientation. However, there is nothing to promote here, nothing to celebrate here without courting disaster. It's more like a pain on the A. that we have to live with.

In the western democratic states 50% of marriage end in divorce. If the trend continues who knows what would happen? Yes I think there is a link with relationships troubles.

2. To diminish individual therefore social crime.

To have individuals able to create what will make them live more authentic life. Relationships where there is always fights, quarrels, is similar to a life in crime where the partners are always in defensive mode, not a situation in which life can be affirmed.

3. And finally to eliminate violence and reduce quarrels to functional level in relationships. Life is dynamic, there are ups and downs, violence is unnecessary.

When Are Relationships Impossible or When Is Separation Inevitable?

It is said that separation defines relationships that oneness obscures it, in that it takes necessarily two separate elements in order to have a link between them, in other words, to have relationships. It is why in this book most of the time the word is written in plural form. When I read that the first time I thought it was "gogligook" a word I use to say that something is meaningless. However, I see Todd, a roommate applying it in his marriage. He seems to be succeeding. Once in a while he left his wife at home alone with the kids for many weeks in business trips. That and other behaviours in the couple suggest they would break up, but instead they are together at least apparently living a normal life. So the insertion of sporadic and spontaneous separations in the life of the couple must be working to keep their relationships alive I personally would not do it that way.

So, according to the paragraph above, stage separation once in while in marriage helps keep it together.

Nonetheless our topic is on separation for good. Here again we have Mr. Sadello and his book *Love and the World* to come to our rescue. I probably have rearranged it to fit this book. According to what I have read in his book separation is unavoidable when:

1. the work to be done together is considered too hard,

2. there are too many conflicts, the work to do together has already been done.

Some men and some women think if the person is not married they will be able to seduce him or her. Very serious mistake. If the person has goals that require a certain type of woman or man. you may succeed in your seduction enterprise, but in the long run hope for troubles, even murder.

Do the folks in Hollywood, persons such as Britney, Jessica Simpson master the concept. I bet they do.

The Benefits of Marriage

In the book called *The Case for Marriage: Why Married People Are Happier, Healthier, and Better off Financially* by Linda Waite and Maggie Gallagher there are underlined the fundamental points of the argumentation on the benefits of marriage which are:

That being married is actually better for you physically, materially and spiritually than being single.

The separation of the material things from the physical things may attract your attention, for some of you may not see a difference between the two groups. But physically can also refer to the body of a person and materially to things. Spiritually refers to the mental world (me I have two different groups incomplete and complete life see Psychokinetic Telepathy for more information).

A simpler way to see it is the substantial and the non-substantial world. This way the substantial covers for the body and the material things.

Anyway, the benefit of marriage is elevated by the two counselors who have long experience in the field of marriage? They speak according to their observation and statistics about the benefit of being married.

That "married couples have better health, live longer, earn more money and accumulate more wealth, feel more fulfilled in their lives, enjoy more satisfying sexual relationships, have more satisfying successful children than those who remain single, cohabit, or get divorced".

This part of the findings on the benefit of marriage reminds me my own observations on successful and unsuccessful relationships which is part of the argumentation in "Relations Amoureuse". Of the two brothers mentioned above the one in a successful relationships or marriage is also more successful finance wise and health wise. Yesterday July 26, 2005 I had to send some money to Arnold, as you guess, the one in the non-successful relationships, knowing that he is not doing well in Florida, far away from his family in New York. I am more worried about him than any one else in the entire family of four brothers, one sister, because he has to live far away from his own family to avoid getting in fight with his wife.

The brother in the successful relationships or marriage, according to the definition of successful relationships we have adopted above is doing so well that his children, one man and two women, are working grown up, but still they refused to move out, are still living in their parents' house. So in one family there is running out in the other there is running in.

Although, I am aware of "The Case for Marriage" only after I have written 7 of the 8 chapters of "Relation Amoureuse"; there is some similarity between the two books. Then, despite that, it is not the reason why I mention *The Case for Marriage* at the end of "Relation Amoureuse". I just want to make sure that the reader of "Relation Amoureuse" is also conscious of the existence of the other book, and because I suspect that some violence in some relationships is the direct result of not being committed in those relationships, but the commitment I have in mind is not necessarily equal to marriage. It may be also cohabitation.

That statistics show, for example, violence is less prevalent in married household and that divorce reduces male life expectancy in the order of-a-pack-a-day-cigarette habit.

We are going to deal with the part of that point on reduced males life expectancy in divorce. Violence less prevalent in married couples will be approached further at the end of the book.

I did make the research in 1993 when I wrote the first version of *Kickitwell or Else* a small book on how to give up an addiction, especially smoking addiction. But according to it tobacco smoking reduced life expectancy of everyone divorce or not divorce, males or females, not just divorced males. Nonetheless, because here we are on benefits of marriage, it is appropriate to intervene with researches on divorce males.

It makes the point between scientific and unscientific observation. For if we were to conclude according to what we hear and see in the news, we would say that violence is more prevalent in married couples. Recently a court from the accusation of having killed his wife acquitted actor Blakeney. Things like that are what we see and hear in the news almost every day. Before Blakeney, there was a certain Peterson, accused of killing his wife also, but he was not acquitted by the court, was rather found guilty and is still in jail. Before him there were OJ Simpson acquitted of the accusation of killing his wife.

It is that, in one hand, for the statistics we take into account a big number of married couples and compare it with the same number of unmarried couples to arrive at the conclusion that there is less violence in married couples. In the other hand, in the business news, the interest is not focused on the positive side of life.

Wednesday night July 27, 2005, in the TV show called "Queer Helping the Straight" there was a military man leaving to go on duty in Iraq. For some reason he had to marry the woman with whom he had already made a child before leaving. So the preparation and the ceremony of the wedding have taken place in very short period of time. During the reception, I couldn't stop tears pouring down from my eyes for no apparent reason. Therefore, yesterday Thursday I was asking myself questions, looking for explanation. I still do not have a clear answer, but I realized that I was like that watching the wedding because I had to start the topic on the benefits of marriage, and, it was the last part of Relation Amoureuse. At first, I thought it could be because the guy was leaving his wife he had just married to go to war.

To include the Creator in your life, sometimes it is sufficient to name it before your activities.

ATA

A.J. Prince has been teaching for many years. He has studied psychology and enjoys his work in it. He has also written several books including "Soul Exposed" volumes 1 through 4, as well as "Jennifer, Nadine, Victoria, and Psychokinetic Telepathy".